Bernese Ob

PATHMASTER GUIDES

CIRCULAR 30 WALKS FROM REGIONAL CENTRES

BERNESE OBERLAND

Maurice & Marion Teal

Series Editor
Richard Sale

The Crowood Press

First published in 1990 by
The Crowood Press Ltd
Gipsy Lane
Swindon
SN2 6DQ

British Library Cataloguing in Publication Data
Teal, Marion
Bernese Oberland. – (Pathmaster guide series).
1. Switzerland – Visitors' guides
I. Title II. Teal, Maurice III. Series
ISBN 1 85223 415 6

Picture Credits
Black and white photographs throughout, and cover photographs all by the authors; all maps by Malcolm Walker.

Acknowledgements
Thanks are due to the Berner Oberland Tourist Office in Interlaken where the staff were kind enough to verify certain facts.

In places times from timetables and certain costs, including fares, have been quoted. These were correct at time of going to press, but it cannot be guaranteed that they will remain the same in subsequent years.

Typeset by Carreg Limited, Nailsea, Bristol
Printed in Great Britain by Redwood Press Ltd, Melksham, Wilts

CONTENTS

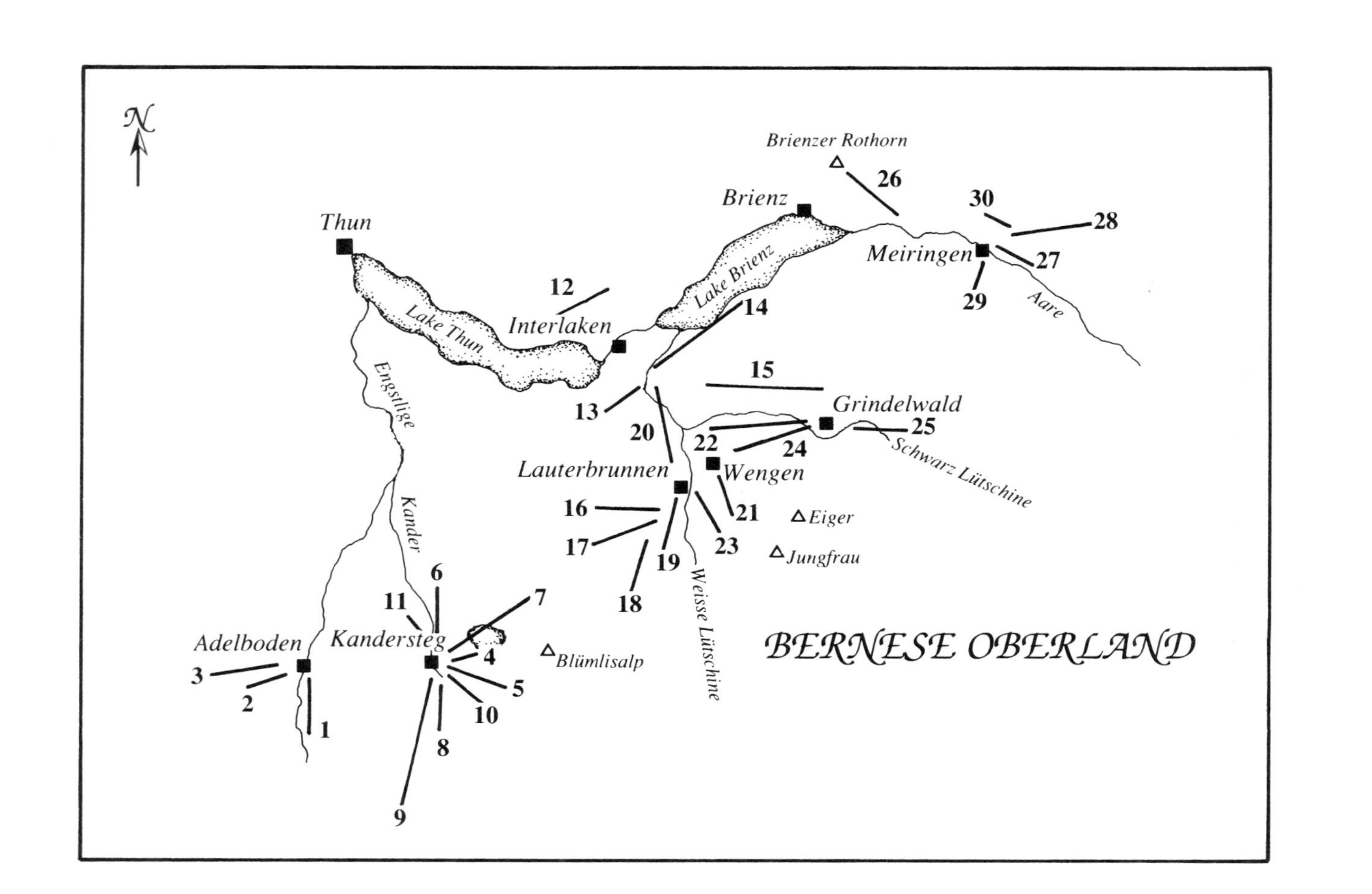
N
Brienzer Rothorn
Thun
Brienz
Meiringen
Lake Thun
Lake Brienz
Interlaken
Aare
Engstlige
Grindelwald
Lauterbrunnen
Wengen
Schwarz Lütschine
Kander
Eiger
Jungfrau
Weisse Lütschine
Adelboden
Kandersteg
Blümlisalp
BERNESE OBERLAND
1
2
3
4
5
6
7
8
9
10
11
12
13
14
15
16
17
18
19
20
21
22
23
24
25
26
27
28
29
30

INTRODUCTION

To think of the Alps is to think of Switzerland, although this great mountain range is spread around several countries. In fact, the only Alpine region that lies entirely within Switzerland is the Bernese Oberland, and the Swiss claim, justifiably, that it is the most beautiful of Alpine groups. Certainly there are few that can match it for variety of scenery.

Its great feature, the so-called 'Wall of the Oberland', can be seen from afar. Rising in the east as the Wetterhorn it extends along a line just south of west through the world-famous peaks of the Eiger, the Monch and the Jungfrau. Further, the series continues over the Blümlisalp, the Doldenhorn and the Balmhorn, then, as the altitude diminishes, the Wildstrubel, Wildhorn and les Diablerets. Other important features of the region are the sizeable lakes of Thun and Brienz. Situated as they are, comparatively close to snowy mountains, they are a fine additional element in the landscape.

The world has become aware of the Bernese Oberland as a holiday playground and some of the credit for this is due to British pioneers. Sir Arnold Lunn popularised skiing, and Alfred Wills is reputed to have started the sport of mountaineering by climbing the Wetterhorn in 1854. Since then British mountaineers have featured in many important climbs.

But you don't have to be a mountaineer to enjoy the Oberland. The region, apart from around the highest peaks, is very much the province of the walker. This book contains descriptions of thirty walks of all types, from gentle afternoon strolls to strenuous high-level tramps. We hope you enjoy them. Among the other sections you will find items of information that may be useful.

The Oberland as a Walking Area

People go walking in their leisure time for a variety of reasons – chiefly perhaps for the exercise, but also, as importantly, to enjoy the scenery through which they are passing.The scenery in the Bernese Oberland is outstanding, making this a superb area for walking. The highest mountains carry a raiment of permanent ice and snow (terrain over which the walks in this book do not go). Only two of the walks here, Number 5 (in the

Gasteretal) and Number 9 (over the Gemmi Pass) penetrate among the high peaks at altitudes below the summer snowline. Most of the others explore the lower ranges just to the north, and from these the great snow and ice mountains feature spectacularly in the landscape.

To enjoy your mountain walking to the full it is sometimes desirable to start your walk some distance from where you are staying and perhaps at an altitude appreciably higher. In fact, you need a form of transport to get you started and maybe to bring you back at the end of the day. Fortunately public transport is good throughout Switzerland, and in the Bernese Oberland it is excellent – probably as good as one could find anywhere in a comparable area. Railways, buses and all kinds of mountain lifts are dealt with more fully under 'Getting About' (pages 20–24).

Swiss countryside is well laid out for walking, with a system that is perhaps better than that of any other country in the world. The Swiss Footpath Protection Association is largely responsible for this, having identified and signposted 35,000km (21,800 miles) of paths and tracks. These are of two categories – the *Wanderweg* and the *Bergweg*. The former is a wide path, generally of good firm surface and not normally of high gradient. A *Bergweg* is a mountain path and can sometimes be found over very rough country. It is invariably narrower than a *Wanderweg*, sometimes *very* narrow, and can be steep and exposed. But it can also be well engineered, with constructed steps and safety cables where deemed necessary.

Signposting in the area is extensive, with the posts sometimes carrying the name and altitude, in metres, of the locality. The pointed portion of the sign is yellow when signifying a *Wanderweg* and white/red/white when pointing the direction of a *Bergweg*. Between signposts paths may be marked by intermediate lozenge-shaped signs or painted flashes in the same colours.

Another endearing aspect of the Oberland as a walking area is the frequency of mountain inns and restaurants, and in this category we include mountain huts. Establishments of this kind are sometimes found in the most unlikely places, perhaps at a time when you would do almost anything for a cup of coffee or a bite to eat. Of course, this state of affairs is not favoured by all people. There are those whose instinct is to head for the wilderness, to whom the sight of a mountain inn or cable car would be anathema, and if you are in this category, perhaps the popular parts of the Alps are not for you. The Oberland is a fine place to be, where you can enjoy the feeling of being in wild places yet remain at the most only hours from the trappings of civilisation – the best of both worlds, in fact.

How the Walks are Organised

The thirty walks featured in this book are based on a number of different resorts, but the public transport systems are so good in the region that a high proportion of the walks can be done from any one of a number of resorts. Wengen, Lauterbrunnen, Stechelberg and Mürren, for example, are so well interconnected that they could be thought of as one centre. Wilderswil is only 18 minutes from Lauterbrunnen by train and Grindelwald less than half an hour. (Incidentally, although only one walk starts from Grindelwald, it should be pointed out that three others finish at this resort.) Mechanical assistance is pretty much a necessity to reach the starting place of several routes and sometimes to return from the finishing point. Not to use public transport would mean extending the walking time considerably, and some routes in this case would simply not be possible for most people.

Of the thirty walks, sixteen can be described as being circular routes, that is, finishing at the starting point, and thirteen are 'A' to 'B'. The Gasteretal walk (Number 5) is a hybrid, the starting place being passed during the return leg. The descriptions of the 'A' to 'B' walks include suggestions on how to return to the starting point, and there are also suggestions as to how to shorten walks and, in one or two cases, how to lengthen them.

Each section dealing with a walk is preceded by details of the map covering the route, an estimated walking time, a grading, and the highest and lowest altitudes of the walk. Before the details of the walk itself is a short preamble giving a brief outline of the route, how to get to the start (where applicable) and perhaps an item or two of interest. For walks that start from a resort, the starting point is the railway station or, where no railway is present, the bus terminus.

The map numbers are those of the Swiss National Survey and are in two series, one of 1:50,000 scale, the other of 1:25,000. They can be obtained in this country from Stanfords, 12–14 Long Acre, London WC2E 9LP. The Wanderkartes, which form the cheapest way of covering the routes, are only obtainable in Switzerland, at tourist information offices, railway stations and many shops. Some are of scales 1:50,000 and 1:33,333 so be wary. Some of the spellings of place names on the maps can be inconsistent too – 'P's sometimes replace 'B's, 'Ch' occasionally takes the place of 'K', and 'X' may be seen where you might expect 'Z'. A sketch map of each route is included in this book.

The walking times quoted were arrived at after comparing our own times with those that appear on official signposts. These, given in terms of 'std' (short for the German word *Stunde* meaning hours), are presented as average walking times but they are not always reliable. Occasionally they appear too long, at times on the short side, and there are instances where the times of two or more shorter distances do not add up to the combined time. Walking time is exactly what it says and doesn't allow for meal times or rest periods.

Included are a number of shorter walks of up to three hours, suitable for a half day. Walks timed at much more than three hours can easily stretch into a full day's outing, especially if you have to travel to the start, or back from the finish. A break for lunch, innumerable stops to take pictures and an extended look at something of interest soon have the clock hands advancing. The Blausee walk is a good example. You can walk to this beauty spot in an hour and a quarter, but if you go in to spend a couple of hours looking round and an hour for lunch, the return walk will not get you back to Kandersteg much before teatime.

Some of the walks described are suitable for a family with quite young children, and for the elderly, while others are more testing and require a reasonable level of physical fitness. Under 'Grading', we have tried to convey the relative difficulties of the walks and in some cases, which parts of a walk are easy and which are more difficult. In Walk Number 19, for example, the path from Grütschalp to Mürren gives pleasant easy walking for the family, whereas the strenuous two-hour climb to Grütschalp might be a bit much for young children or an elderly person.The grading has been given to two components: the degree of physical effort needed, and the amount of exposure to very steep, sometimes precipitous ground. Under the former, 'easy' would represent wide paths, generally level or with low gradients. A 'strenuous' route would include at least one long climb at high gradient or be over fairly rough terrain, while 'moderate' walks could contain shorter passages of steep ascent. Grading of exposure is more difficult. In a certain situation that one person would describe as 'exposed', another would be completely unaffected. Also, in many places where exposure exists, mountain paths are provided with cables. The width of a path comes into the reckoning, of course. The Geissweg (near Adelboden) or the Gemmi path are not described as exposed, even though terrifying drops are only feet away, because the paths are comfortably wide and protected with safety cables. The aim here is to convey the relative exposure without being too alarmist!

The values given for maximum and minimum altitude are not intended to tell you the amount of ascent or descent, but to present an idea of what's involved and as a point of interest.

The walk descriptions are straightforward and should be easily understandable. Each move is included, even though there is probably a signpost on the spot. There are bound to be junctions without a signpost, and quite often the destination that you are looking for is not mentioned.

How to Get There

By Air

The nearest airport to the Bernese Oberland is at Berne, but only Dan-Air operate a scheduled service there, flying from Gatwick. Zurich is much more used, with Swissair flying from Heathrow, Manchester and Birmingham, British Airways from Heathrow, Dan-Air from Gatwick and Aer Lingus from Dublin. The only other airport that could be considered is Geneva which is used by British Airways, flying from Heathrow, Gatwick and Manchester, and Air Europe from Gatwick. Air Europe has some quite competitive fares in early and late season and this could be a good reason for flying to Geneva. If you hold a Swiss Card (*see* 'Getting About') you can travel by rail free from the airport to your chosen resort (and return). So which airport you use is less important, except that Geneva is further – but not that much further away – from the Oberland than Zurich, and the journey takes from 1/2 hour to 1 hour longer.

If you are proceeding by rail from Zurich or Geneva airports you might like to take advantage of the Fly-rail baggage scheme. There is a charge for each item of luggage and all your baggage is delivered to your destination within an hour or two of your own arrival. A leaflet giving full details is available from the Swiss National Tourist Office.

You can, of course, hire a car in advance and arrange to pick it up at the airport. Thomas Cook is one company which operates such a scheme.

By Rail

Arrangements are best made through your travel agent, who will reserve such accommodation as you need on the cross-Channel ferry and Continental railways. You may, for instance, require sleeping berths or couchettes on the train. If you travel from London (Victoria) to Dover or Folkestone for a ferry to Calais, your route on the other side is likely to be via Lille and Strasbourg to Basle, then via Berne to the resort of your choice. If you take the ferry from Newhaven to Dieppe, your route will probably be via Paris, Dijon, Pontarlier, Les Verrières (frontier), Neuchâtel and Berne. On all these services there are 1st and 2nd classes. If you have a Swiss Card (*see* 'Getting About') you travel free from the frontier station onward (and return).

A Rail Europe Family Card, obtainable from British Rail, gives fare reductions to a family travelling to Switzerland. Full-time students and scholars with a valid international Student/Scholar Identity Card, or under 26 years old, can obtain reduced-rate tickets from STA Travel, 74 Old Brompton Road, London SW7 3LH (tel: 071 581 8233), and 117 Euston Road, London NW1 2SX. Also, if the traveller is under 26 years, tickets can be bought from Eurotrain, 52 Grosvenor Gardens, London SW1W 0AG (tel: 071 730 6525) and Transalpino, 71 Buckingham Palace Road, London SW1W 0QL (tel: 071 834 9656). If you are aged 60 or over and hold a British Rail Senior Citizen Railcard you can purchase a Rail Europe Senior Card. With this, it is possible to obtain up to 50 per cent discount on railway tickets in Belgium, France, Luxembourg, the Netherlands, and on most Swiss railways. Also you can have up to 50 per cent discount on British Rail when you buy a through international rail/sea ticket. However, these reductions do not apply to sleeping accommodation or to travel by Motorail (except in some cases to passenger fare only). Rail Europe Senior Cards can be purchased at British Rail Travel Centres or from European Rail appointed travel agents. They are valid for up to a year (validity period cannot exceed that of your BR Senior Citizen Railcard).

Motorail

If you hate the thought of a long drive on Continental roads, the idea of Motorail might appeal. Unfortunately, Motorail services to the Alps are limited. One from Brussels to Brig, in the Rhône Valley, operates from May to September, from once to three times a week. This is an eleven-hour journey and having arrived at Brig you would need to put the vehicle on to the local car train to go back through the Loschberg Tunnel to Kandersteg. French railways run Motorail services from Paris to Lyon and Paris to St Gervais throughout the year. Both these leave some driving to be done at the other end.

By Road

If you are considering driving to the Bernese Oberland there are a number of things you will have to do in advance; these are largely dealt with under 'Before you Go'. Your car ferry tickets will depend partly on which route you prefer and partly where you live. P & O operate the most ferries – Dover to Boulogne, Calais, Ostend or Zeebrugge, Portsmouth to Cherbourg or Le Havre, and Felixstowe to Zeebrugge. Sealink run Folkstone/Boulogne,

Harwich/Hook of Holland, Newhaven/Dieppe, Portsmouth/Cherbourg and Weymouth/Cherbourg. Brittany Ferries offer Plymouth/Roscoff, Poole/Cherbourg, Portsmouth/Caen, Portsmouth/St Malo and Cork/Roscoff. Of the others, North Sea Ferries operate from Hull to Rotterdam and Zeebrugge, while the Sally Line run Ramsgate/Dunkerque and the Olau Line, Sheerness/Vlissingen. In addition hovercraft services from Dover to Calais and Boulogne are run by Hoverspeed.

Which route you follow onwards depends on whether you want to use motorways or ordinary roads, bearing in mind that most French autoroutes are toll roads and a road tax is payable on Swiss motorways. To go all the way on motorways, the best ports to start from would be Hook, Rotterdam, Vlissingen and possibly Ostend or Zeebrugge. From these you head east, then make for Cologne and follow the autobahn system up the Rhine Valley to Basle, then on to Berne. On these routes the motorways as far as the Swiss frontier are free.

From Le Havre and Caen you can drive virtually all the way by autoroute, via Paris to Besançon then on ordinary roads via Neuchâtel to Berne. From Dunkerque, Calais and Boulogne there is a choice between a mixture of motorway and trunk roads or all the way by trunk roads. In either case, head for St Quentin then proceed via Rheims, Langres and Besançon, then on to Berne via Neuchâtel. If you prefer quieter roads, head for Cambrai then go via Sedan, Verdun, Neufchâteau, Belfort, Porrentruy and Biel, to Berne.

Driving from Dieppe, you can either go south to join the autoroute system at Rouen, or go on ordinary roads via Beauvais, Rheims and Chaumont to Belfort, thus avoiding Paris. Drivers from Le Havre could also go this way. From Caen, an alternative to the motorway route would be via Chartres, Sens, Troyes, Chaumont and Belfort. Motorists using ferries to Cherbourg can drive to Caen then use one of the suggested routes from there. From St Malo either go south to Rennes, picking up the autoroute there to go just south of Paris on the way to Besançon, or on ordinary roads via Alençon to Chartres. Motorists landing at Roscoff are faced with a long drive. They can head east by way of Dinan and Alençon to Chartres and onwards as previously suggested, or go to Rennes and use the autoroutes.

Drivers should always carry their driving licence. A current full UK licence is recognised in Germany, France and Switzerland. You are advised also to carry the appropriate Vehicle Registration Document, unless it is a hired vehicle, in which case you require a Vehicle on Hire Certificate, obtainable from one or other of the motoring organisations.

Certain regulations have to be observed when driving on the Continent. In France, Belgium, the Netherlands and Switzerland, the minimum age for driving is 18, and in France you can only drive in excess of 90kph (56 mph) if your full licence is at least a year old. Seat belts must be worn, where fitted, and in France no child under 10 years of age is allowed to sit in the front seat of a vehicle. In the other relevant countries, the minimum age for sitting in a front seat is 12 years. Headlamp beam converters or deflectors should be fitted for driving on the right. It is advisable to have yellow headlamps if you are going to drive at night in France, and this conversion is easily achieved by applying 'headlamp yellow lacquer'. Dipped headlamps must be used in tunnels and should be used in heavy rain or poor visibility. In Switzerland, driving with sidelights only is not permitted under any circumstance. Motorcyclists must use dipped headlights at all times, day or night, when travelling through Belgium or France.

An advance warning triangle must be carried by all vehicles in all the relevant countries, in case of breakdown. It is also advisable to have wing mirrors on both sides of your vehicle.

Speed limits vary from country to country. On motorways the maximum speed is 120kph (75 mph) in Belgium, the Netherlands, Luxembourg and Switzerland, and 130kph (81 mph) in France and West Germany. In built-up areas the maximum speed is 50kph (31 mph) in the Netherlands and Switzerland, and 60kph (37 mph) in Belgium, France, Luxembourg and West Germany. On other roads the limit is 80kph (50 mph) in the Netherlands and Switzerland, and 90kph (56 mph) in the other countries. There are restrictions on towing trailers but these depend on weight; in Switzerland, for example, caravans and trailers up to a ton in weight are restricted to 80kph (50 mph).

Swiss traffic police are authorised to collect fines on the spot for offences concerning speed limits, lighting and seat belts.

Although the equivalent of 2-star petrol is still obtainable in some countries, lead-free petrol is becoming increasingly available. Look out for '*Bleifrei*' (German) or '*essence sans plomb*' (French).

Motor Coaches

Fares are competitive in the high season, but there is only one well-known service. This is from London to Geneva, operated by Eurolines of 52 Grosvenor Gardens, Victoria, London SW1. Details can be obtained and bookings made at National Express offices.

Terrain and Climate

The Bernese Oberland is sometimes said to extend from Lake Geneva in the west to Goschenen in the east. The most dramatic terrain, though, is found in approximately the middle third of this region and it is here that most of the walks described in this book are concentrated.

This mountainous mass is bounded on the south by the Rhône Valley but the boundary between the canton of Berne and the canton of Valais is along the watershed, over the highest peaks. Almost all the walks, then, are north of this boundary. Only one, Walk Number 9 to the Gemmi Pass and down to Leukerbad, crosses it, but we felt that this route couldn't be omitted.The highest peaks, which include the Jungfrau, the Monch, the Eiger and the highest, the Finsteraarhorn, are along or near the watershed. This is a region of perpetual ice and snow; the Aletsch Glacier, the longest in the Alps, is here. Although some of the walks described here go up to the very edge of glaciers, they do not venture on to them. Glaciers and snowfields can be walked on, but for the most part they remain the province of the Alpinist.

To the north of the higher mountains, ridge upon ridge of lesser peaks run down towards the two large lakes of Thun and Brienz. Between the ridges are deep-cut valleys, with villages in the bottom and on the flanks, some of which have developed into holiday resorts. The Engstligental has Adelboden on its northern flank and Kandersteg nestles in the Kandertal. The Lauterbrunnental has Lauterbrunnen in its bottom, with Wengen and Mürren perched on either flank, while Grindelwald is found near the head of the Lütschental.

In the eastern part of the Oberland the Haslital, through which the river Aare flows, forms a deep trench through the mountains up to the Grimsel Pass. Some regard this as the limit of the Bernese Oberland, but there are high peaks to the east of it, while to the north are further rocky ridges. Here is the northern limit of the canton of Berne. During Walks 26 and 28 you actually follow the canton boundary and the latter route enters the canton of UnterWalden for a short distance in the neighbourhood of Tannen. To the north of the lakes of Thun and Brienz are the spiny ridges of the Sigristwilergrat, the Guggisgrat and the Riedergrat, all of which are really part of the Bernese Oberland region.

In general the limit of trees is at about 2,000m (6,560ft) with the snow line averaging 2,600m (8,528ft) in summer. In between, where the terrain is not rocky, are the true Alps, used by the Swiss as pastureland.

The lakes are major geographical features. They blend beautifully with the mountain scene and help to make the Oberland such an outstanding holiday playground. Lake Thun, with a length of approximately 18.5km ($11^{1}/_{2}$ miles) and an average width of almost 3 km (2 miles) is at 558m (1,831ft) above sea level. Lake Brienz is 6m higher and 14km ($8^3/_4$ miles) long by 2.5km ($1^1/_2$ miles) wide. One of the walks (Number 14) is largely along its shore.

As with the majority of mountain ranges the weather in the Alps can be variable. In summer it is generally quite good, but exposed as the mountains are to moist air currents flowing from the Atlantic, a certain amount of precipitation is to be expected. In this respect the Bernese Oberland is at rather a disadvantage. Being the most north-westerly of the Swiss Alps, it is first in line to be assailed by storms from the west. Consequently, precipitation is higher in the Oberland than in ranges further south and east. Nevertheless there can be reasonably long sunny spells in the mountains. It is estimated that in an average year, precipitation can be expected on about ten days of each of the summer months. During the fine spells it can be quite hot and this can give rise to thunderstorms. These usually break in mid to late afternoon. July is the month when this is most likely, and has on average seven thundery days. In many resorts weather forecasts are displayed outside post offices, and sometimes in railway stations.

The 'walking season' in the Bernese Oberland is generally regarded as extending from May to the end of September. Outside of this period, a combination of snow, ice and shorter days render many of the routes doubtful, indeed, inadvisable propositions. Some of the high routes, for example, Walks 7, 15 and 17, may not be feasible until July. Tourist information offices may be able to advise on the condition of these high paths. When exactly you go to the Oberland within the period suggested depends on a number of factors. You may favour May because there is more snow and this would look good in your photographs, while June and July are best for the display of wild flowers. In late August and September the number of tourists drops off and this is the time of least snow on the high routes. Another factor you might consider is that mountain inns and restaurants only start to open in late June for their short season and will be closed by mid-September.

Accommodation

Across the Bernese Oberland accommodation can be found to suit all tastes. This can range from four and five star hotels to camping or *Matratzenlager* dormitories.

Hotels and Pensions

Most resorts boast four or five star hotels where rooms may cost up to £140 a day, or even more. The majority of hotel dwellers would settle for two and three star establishments where costs are likely to be in the £25 – £50 per day range. Pensions are smaller hotels, usually rated at one or two star, and priced at £15 – £30 per day. There are plenty to choose from. Wengen has twenty-eight hotels and pensions, Adelboden twenty-six, Grindelwald forty-six, Kandersteg twenty-five, Lauterbrunnen twelve, Meiringen thirty-seven, Mürren thirteen and Wilderswil fifteen. In Interlaken, at the hub of the Oberland, there are no less than seventy-one hotels and pensions. You might also consider Frutigen (in the Kandertal), with ten hotels, Stechelberg with four, and Zweilütschinen with one.

If you want to visit during the high season it is advisable to book your accommodation in advance. This can be done directly with the hotel or through a travel agent, and the Swiss National Tourist Office can provide a list of agents in the UK who represent Swiss hotels. Visitors who have not booked rooms can get advice from local tourist offices.

Youth Hostels

If you are a member of your own national youth hostels organisation, perhaps the Youth Hostels Association of England and Wales (YHA) or Scottish Youth Hostels Association (SYHA), you can seek accommodation at Swiss hostels, but only if you are under twenty-five years of age. Older hostellers can be admitted if there is room, but this precludes booking in advance. Younger people who wish to reserve accommodation are requested to give at least five days' notice of arrival. In the Bernese Oberland there are hostels at Grindelwald, Gimmelwald (near Mürren), Bonigen (near Interlaken), Brienz, and Meiringen. There is also one sharing a building with a *Berghaus* at Tannen, right on the line of Walk 28. The International Youth Hostel Handbook is useful, and can be obtained from YHA Travel, 14 Southampton Street, London WC2E 7HY, or SYHA, 7 Glebe Crescent, Stirling FK8 2JA.

Also worth mentioning here is Balmers Herberge of Interlaken. This is best described as a private hostel and is very popular with young tourists.

Chalets and Apartments

There is a surprising amount of self-catering accommodation in the Bernese Oberland, and in some resorts the number of beds in this category outnumbers those in hotels. Much has been created for the winter skiing season and is available for summer visitors.

Apartments are by far the most numerous, each being fully furnished. The beds are equipped with bed linen, duvets and pillows and in the kitchens are crockery, cutlery and cooking utensils. Towels are generally supplied and changed every week, together with bed linen, tea towels and tablecloths. A refrigerator and cooking stove are standard equipment, but not often a TV.

You can book an apartment yourself or through an agent. If you decide to do it yourself, write to the tourist information office of the chosen resort, giving details of what you require, and not forgetting an international reply coupon. They will send you a list of a number of apartments with names, addresses and telephone numbers of the landlords and a card with sections printed in German and English. You fill in the card and send it to the landlord of the apartment that you choose.

If you would rather book through an agent, send to the Swiss Tourist Office for a list of contacts. Chalets and apartments can also be reserved through Interhome Limited, 383 Richmond Road, Twickenham, Middlesex TW1 2EF (tel: 081 891 1294).

Camping

Not only is camping the least expensive way of exploring the Oberland, it is in many ways the most convenient. With a tent and particularly with a caravan it is much easier to switch from resort to resort. Motor caravans have the additional advantage of taking up less space than a caravan plus car, or a tent plus car, and this is useful in high season when sites tend to become crowded.

Turn-around times are often short on sites, as some people stay only one or two nights. The best time to get into a campsite is about ten or eleven o'clock in the morning. Have patience and avoid changing sites at weekends. It is possible to reserve pitches in advance at some sites, but this nullifies the advantage of mobility enjoyed by the camper.

The backpacker, of course, has few worries about moving from place to place. With his small tent he can often find a space even on a crowded site, and can resort to wild camping if all else fails.

Campsites in Switzerland are generally of good standard but charges are on the high side, much higher than in France, for example. They are invariably clean and you can usually get a shower (although you should be prepared to pay for it). In the Oberland the sites tend to be rather small, as you might expect in mountainous terrain.

Adelboden has two sites, both quite small, near the main road before the town is reached. Kandersteg has only one site, the 'Rendezvous' near to the Oeschinensee chairlift station. Grindelwald has five, all in the valley below the town, or on the opposite side of the valley. There are no campsites at Mürren or Wengen, but Lauterbrunnen has two and Stechelberg, further up the valley, two more. Three of the latter four are bigger than the Oberland average. Wilderswil has a site in the middle of the village and there is another, the 'Jungfraublick' between Wilderswil and Interlaken. There are five in the Meiringen area, all clustered around Innertkirchen which is about $2^1/_2$ miles up the river Aare.

Camping guides are published by the Swiss Camping and Caravanning Federation and the Swiss Camping Association, and can be purchased from the Swiss National Tourist Office.

Mountain Huts and Inns

The routes described in this book are aimed primarily at walkers who would be staying in one or other of the resorts. On the other hand, many of the routes go past or near to mountain huts and inns, and circumstances such as the unexpected onset of bad weather might compel a walker to seek the services offered by these establishments. This cannot be ruled out for walkers tackling, say, the Hohtürli or the high-level route over the Faulhorn. A visitor might also like to sample the atmosphere of a mountain inn 'deliberately', and split a walk into two leisurely halves.

Accommodation in the mountain huts is always of the dormitory type (*Matratzenlager*), with no segregation of the sexes. Each visitor is allocated a mattress space and provided with pillow and blankets, but no sheets. Mountain inns also offer this type of accommodation but have a number of private rooms as well. Both huts and inns provide meals, except some smaller and more remote huts.

Overleaf are some of the huts and inns passed by the walking routes in this book.

Walk	Locality	Name of hut or inn
5	Selden (Gasteretal)	Hotel Gasteretal
5	Selden (Gasteretal)	Hotel Steinbock
5	Selden (Gasteretal)	Berghaus Heimritz
7	Hohtürli	Blümlisalp Hutte
9	Gemmi	Berghotel Schwarenbach
10	Gemmi	Doldenhornhutte
15	Faulhorn	Hotel Faulhorn
16	Poganggen	Rotstockhutte
18	Obersteinberg	Berghotel Tschingelhorn
18	Obersteinberg	Hotel Obersteinberg

It is worth pointing out that dormitory-type accommodation is also available at some hotels in the resorts.

Getting About

If you have motored down from a Channel port you will presumably have your car available for some of your local journeys. All the main valleys have roads up them and the road surfaces are generally beyond reproach. In the Engstligental you can drive beyond Adelboden to Unter dem Birg at the foot of the Engstligenalp cableway. The road up the Kandertal goes to Kandersteg and beyond to Eggenschwand, where Stock cableway starts. In the Lauterbrunnental the road penetrates to Stechelberg, passing the lower station of the Schilthorn cableway. However, you cannot drive to Wengen or Mürren, because these holiday villages are car-free. The road to Grindelwald, up the Lütschental, is an excellent one, and Meiringen is only just off the main highway up the Haslital. Petrol pumps can be found in most towns and villages.

The adventurous motorist will doubtless find lesser roads that penetrate even deeper into the mountains but surfaces are rough and some may be toll roads. One of these is the Gasteretal road that carries on from the public road at Eggeschwand. This goes as far as Selden from where you could do a version of Walk 5.

You can, of course, hire a car in Switzerland (*see* under 'How to Get There'). However, if you are not taking your own vehicle (or even if you are) you may prefer to consider one or other of the travel cards, of which more at the end of this section.

Of the 30 walks described in this book there are thirteen in which the start is not reached by public road. From fourteen you would normally seek transport to return from the finishing point, so, even if you have a vehicle at your disposal you would still need public transport. Fortunately, Switzerland's excellent transport system makes it possible for the visitor to reach points that are miles from and thousands of feet above the nearest road. The Swiss rail network forms the basis of it, and you can travel by train to most resorts. There are also cable cars, chairlifts, gondola lifts, funicular railways, cog railways, PTT buses and lake steamers. It is possible to obtain a free timetable of all these systems in the Bernese Oberland in tourist information centres. This interesting and useful booklet is available from May onwards.

Almost as important as the railway system are the Postauto buses operated by the PTT (Postal, Telegraph and Telephone Service). These run to many places not accessible by rail, such as Adelboden; passengers change from train to bus at Frutigen. It is also possible to travel between Grindelwald and Meiringen by way of the Grosse Scheidegg, changing at Schwarzwaldalp. Use of PTT buses is suggested in several of the walks in this book. The vehicles are painted an instantly recognisable yellow and have a characteristic horn sound which is much used on the many hairpin bends that are encountered. This is to warn other drivers, for PTT buses have the right of the road at all times and can keep to the inside of sharp bends. Extremely safe, with three independent braking systems, the buses are all in the hands of expert drivers.

Of the cable car systems (*Luftseilbahnen* in German, *téléphérique* in French) the most famous is that of the Schilthorn. There are four stages – Stechelberg to Gimmelwald, Gimmelwald to Mürren, Mürren to Birg and Birg to Schilthorn summit. These run every half an hour and on three stages 100 passengers can be carried. The Wengen to Männlichen cable car could be used to start Walk 24 and by the less energetic to do part of Walk 21. This runs every 15 minutes in the tourist season. If you do Walk 9 you will be using two cable cars – the Eggeschwand–Stock and the Leukerbad–Gemmi. Both of these operate every half-hour. Other cable cars in the area include Grindelwald–Pfingstegg, Unter dem Birg–Engstligenalp, Sandweidli–Isenfluh (in the Lauterbrunnen valley) and Kandersteg–Allmenalp. The last two are unconnected with any walk in this book, but they could be useful in other endeavours.

Chairlifts (*Sesselbahnen* or *télésièges*) are a useful form of transport for the mountain walker and a very pleasant one when the weather is kind. They have an advantage over cable cars in that they are continuously moving during their hours of operation, so you don't have to wait until a set time. Their main drawback is that they are open to the elements, although passengers are given protective clothing to wear when the weather is bad. When conditions deteriorate beyond a certain point the system may be stopped, after ensuring, of course, that no one is stranded between stations! Recommended for use with some of the walks in this book are Kandersteg–Oeschinensee (a double-chair system), Beatenberg–Neiderhorn (double), Stock–Sunnbüel (single chairs), and Grindelwald–First (double), at present the longest chairlift in Europe. Other chairlifts in the area include Adelboden–Schwarzenfeld, Melchsee Frutt–Balmeregghorn and Magisalp–Planplatten (this is the top component of the Meiringen–Planplatten system).

Gondola lifts, also known as *Gondelbahnen* and *télécabines*, are similar to chairlifts except that enclosed gondolas, usually holding four people, are used instead of chairs. The Grindelwald–Mannlichen system is the longest in Europe at 6.2km (nearly 4 miles) and could be used in conjunction with Walk 24. Plans are afoot to convert the Grindelwald–First cableway to a *Gondelbahn*, but this project will not be completed before the winter of 1991–92. Until then the system will continue to operate as a chairlift. Other gondola lifts include Twing–Kasserstatt and Reuti–Magisalp, the middle two sections of the Meiringen–Planplatten system.

Mountain railways where carriages are hauled up an incline by a cable are called funiculars (*Drahtseilbahnen* in German). The carriages are usually operated in pairs, each one going in the opposite direction to the other, over the same rails with a double track at half-way where the two pass each other. Gradients can be up to 1 in $1^1/_2$. The most important funicular to the walker in the Bernese Oberland is Lauterbrunnen–Grütschalp which runs every 15 minutes. Others include Mürren–Allmendhubel, Lake Brienz–Reichenbach Falls, Beatenbucht (on Lake Thun)–Beatenberg, Interlaken–Harderkulm and Mulenen to the summit of the Niesen (the last two being unconnected with any walk in this book).

Cogwheel railways are also known as rack and pinion railways (*Dampfzahnradbahnen*). The trains are propelled by a toothed wheel operating in a toothed rail, and gradients in the Oberland are up to 1 in 4. (The Pilatus railway near Lucerne actually reaches nearly 1 in 2, the steepest anywhere for this type of railway.) Parts of the national rail system use this system, including the lines connecting Lauterbrunnen to Wengen, Kleine Scheidegg and Grindelwald, and the main rail route to Lucerne over the Brünig Pass. Elsewhere, cogwheel railways are found between Wilderswil and Schynige Platte and on the Brienzer Rothorn. Although not used for any walk in this book, perhaps the most famous cogwheel railway is the one up to the Jungfraujoch. Tunnelling through the rock of the Eiger and the Monch, it climbs to its terminus at 3,454m (11,333ft). This is an excursion no one should miss, but you must pick a good day for it.

Level railways that operate in a conventional manner are known as 'adhesion railways'. There are two of this type in the Bernese Oberland that deserve a mention. One connects with the Grütschalp funicular and takes passengers on to Mürren and back, while the other plies between Meiringen and Innertkirchen and is useful to anyone staying or camping near the latter village. Both these employ single cars; you could call them trams.

Steamers move up and down lakes Thun and Brienz, visiting a variety of ports of call. This form of transport is suggested for returning from Walk 14, and it could also be employed (together with the Beatenbucht–Beatenberg funicular) to reach the start of Walk 12, and perhaps also Walk 26.

Public transport in Switzerland, however good, has to be paid for. Fortunately there are a number of passes and cards that make travelling much less expensive. The Swiss Pass entitles the holder to unlimited travel on railways, boats and most postal buses, and 25 per cent discount on many cablecars, funiculars, and so on. 1989 prices were:

Time Period	2nd Class	1st Class
4 days	£64.00	£94.00
8 days	£78.00	£112.00
15 days	£94.00	£134.00
1 month	£130.00	£186.00

The Swiss Card allows free travel from a frontier railway station or airport to any destination within Switzerland and return. It also allows 50 per cent discount on any excursions taken. (A minority of cableways allow only a smaller discount than this, ranging from 16 per cent–50 per cent.) For one month the 2nd class charge was £40 in 1989 and the 1st class £50.

The Swiss Half Fare Travel Card allows 50 per cent discount on excursions taken and again a smaller discount on some cableways. For one month this cost £26 in 1989.

A Family Card can be obtained free of charge from the Swiss National Tourist Office or any Swiss railway station. It can be used with a full fare ticket or either of the three cards and passes mentioned above to obtain free travel for children aged 6–16, and half fare travel for unmarried offspring aged 16–25.

The Swiss Pass, Swiss Card or Swiss Half Fare Travel Card should be obtained from the Swiss National Tourist Office or through a travel agent before you travel to Switzerland.

A Regional Pass for the Bernese Oberland can be purchased in Switzerland. This is valid for 15 days and entitles the holder to free travel anywhere within the area on any of five days. On the remaining 10 days, travel is subject to 50 per cent discount. The cost in 1989 was £44 for 2nd class and £57 for 1st class, both subject to 20 per cent discount for holders of a Swiss Card and 50 per cent discount for children aged 6–16.

The choice seems bewildering, but if you intend to spend most of your days walking and you need rail travel from an airport or frontier station to your resort then a Swiss Card seems to be the most suitable. If you don't need rail travel to your resort then the Swiss Half Fare Travel Card will be the best choice. However, if you intend not to walk on at least five days but to travel around instead, you might consider a Regional Pass. The Swiss Pass is really for people who want to travel extensively throughout Switzerland.

Money

Presumably you will purchase travellers cheques or obtain Eurocheques before making the journey to Switzerland, but it is wise to change some sterling into Swiss currency and if possible to carry some small change. Swiss banknotes are in denominations of SFr 10, SFr 20, SFr 50, SFr 100, SFr 500 and SFr 1,000. Coins can be to the value of SFr $^1/_2$, SFr 1, SFr 2 and SFr 5, and 5, 10 and 20 centimes.

Travellers cheques, obtainable from travel agents, banks and some building societies, may be in units of pounds sterling, but if you are worried about the value of international currencies it might be safer to buy them in Swiss franc units. These are accepted at their face value and no deductions are made. Travellers cheques in sterling or any other foreign currency can be cashed in a bank or in any official exchange office; these are found at airports, principal railway stations or frontier posts. The current rate of exchange is paid, less commission. Large hotels will generally exchange travellers cheques but usually charge more commission.

Banking hours in Switzerland from Monday to Friday are 8am till 12 noon and 2pm till 5pm. In July and August banks open on Saturdays from 8am till 11.30am.

Any British bank with whom you have an account will supply Eurocheques. These you write yourself for settling bills, making purchases, or obtaining currency from a bank, presenting them with a Eurocheque Card. Each cheque is guaranteed to an approximate value of £100, so if the amount is more than this you will need to write more than one cheque.

If you have National Girobank 'Postcheques' you can obtain currency at Swiss Post Offices, but here again you will need to show your cheque guarantee card.

Although it is advisable to carry some currency, you can make purchases with credit cards. Access, Visa, American Express and Diners Club cards are recognised widely and can be used to pay bills in most hotels (not mountain inns), and larger restaurants. However, they are not generally accepted by petrol filling stations where cash is preferred. At automatic filling stations, SFr 10 and SFr 20 notes are required to operate the dispensers.

This section concerning money would not be complete if it did not mention tipping. In Switzerland the procedure is to include a service charge in the price, whether for a meal or a drink in an hotel or restaurant, at the hairdresser, or in a taxi. This is almost universally 15 per cent so if you add an additional tip to this you will certainly be tipping generously! If the service has been really excellent, you can leave small change, if there is any, but this is not expected. It is however, customary to tip porters.

Walking in the Oberland

There are certain rules that should be observed when walking in Switzerland, as indeed there are in any country. In general, if you leave things as you found them, you cannot go wrong. Close any gate that you have to open. Similarly, with a type of stile that has removable cross members, if you take any out in order to cross the stile, replace them afterwards.

You may occasionally find a picnic site that has provision for making a fire. For safety's sake it is best not to start one in any other circumstances. Starting one in a forbidden area is punishable by law.

Do not leave litter lying about. Take yours back with you until you find an appropriate disposal bin. Remember that items of rubbish left on pastureland could cause harm to grazing cattle. The dumping of garbage in the woods or in rivers is punishable by law.

When walking on steep ground be careful not to dislodge stones, as there may be people or animals below. In the Oberland you can walk wherever there is a path, but you should always keep to the path if you can. Avoid walking through high grass and do not climb over fences. Wherever there is a path, a way past a fence is always provided. This may be a gate, a turnstile, a stile with removable members, or a *Viehgatter*, which is a narrow gap between a single post and a 'vee'. Ladder stiles are sometimes encountered, but the 'climb-over' stile found everywhere in the UK is seldom if ever seen.

Enjoy the wild flowers but do not pick them. The digging up and mass picking of Alpine plants is forbidden. Certain plants are protected species and details of these are widely publicised on posters; they include lady's slipper, edelweiss, martagon (Turk's cap), creeping forget-me-not, tiger lily and all types of orchid. Picking any of these in particular is punishable by law.

There are also points to observe that affect the safety and enjoyment of yourself and your party. Before you start out on a walk, particularly a strenuous one, check the physical condition of your companions, especially children. Do they suffer from vertigo, for example? On the walk, do not start off at too rapid a pace, as this will lead to eventual exhaustion. Keep to a steady plod and it's surprising what progress you make. Rhythm is the important factor. Keep this going even if it means marking time with one foot when making an awkward step. The speed of any party should always be that of the slowest member.

If it's at all possible, before starting a long walk, let someone know which route you intend to take and when you expect to be back.

Clothing and Equipment

The most important items that any walker has to consider are his or her boots. It goes without saying that these must be comfortable and light. 'Climbing' boots are generally heavy, and the soles are too stiff for the kind of walking that we are considering. In recent years the lightweight boot has made its appearance and these really are ideal for walkers. Weighing 1–1.2kg (2–2$^1/_2$lb) per pair they compare favourably with some mountaineering boots that can be more than twice as heavy, and they need little or no breaking in. A good walking boot should be waterproof and have a moulded rubber sole, of Vibram or similar. Despite their numerous advantages, it must be said that boots in this category are not really suitable for snow conditions. They will be all right for the occasional short passage that you might encounter on high-level routes, but not for continuous walking on snowfields and glaciers. However, such extreme conditions are outside the scope of this book.

For shorter walks at low levels, good stout shoes are quite adequate. As a general rule shoes may be worn, if preferred, on paths graded as *Wanderwegs*, but if you are taking to the mountain tracks (or *Bergwegs*), wear boots.

Almost as important as boots are socks. Some people still wear two pairs, and if you do, do not forget to allow for this when buying your boots. Many walkers are quite happy with one pair, while others wear a thin inner pair with thicker socks outside them. Get loop-stitched socks for the most comfort.

Breeches are probably the most useful lower garment to wear for all conditions – the Swiss themselves favour them, and who's to say that they're wrong? In summer, when the weather's fine, warm and reasonably settled, there is no reason why shorts should not be worn. In fact, they will be much more comfortable in the heat of a summer's day.

What you wear above depends on the weather and personal preference, but you should always carry an extra pullover or two in your pack. Remember, it can be much cooler high up than it is in the valley.

Another must is waterproof and windproof clothing. At the very least you should carry a full-length cagoule with a hood, preferably in a bright colour. Over-trousers are not essential, but it is not a bad idea to have them if you think the weather is doubtful. In these days of breathable fabrics, these garments need not be over heavy. Instead of over-trousers (or as well as) you could consider gaiters that cover the tops of your boots.

A rucksack is a most important item, and it is pointless to buy one that is too big. If you are going out for a day's walking all you need to carry, apart from the items mentioned above, are food, maps, water bottle, first aid kit, compass, mitts and bivvy-bag, and perhaps a camera. Get a sack with an external pocket or two, as these are useful for such things as the water bottle and first aid kit. Also, make sure the shoulder straps are well padded.

It is a good idea to carry a pair of mitts. Woollen ones are adequate in the summer months, but for colder conditions you will probably need mitts that are windproof and fairly waterproof. You should also consider a sun-hat. In high summer the Alpine sun can be quite hot and bright, so dark glasses could be useful too. The user of this book will probably not be walking extensively over snow, but some of the high-level routes may take you near to the snowfields and glaciers where the glare is certainly appreciable.

Carry a map and a compass. The description of each walk will tell you which maps cover the route in question. It is an advantage to carry these items in a transparent waterproof case. The most useful type of compass is one built into a transparent base that has a straight edge.

A bivvy-bag should be included in your rucksack for the protection of anyone disabled by some unfortunate circumstances. This is an extremely light item and will take up little space. Similarly, you should not forget a first aid kit in a party of walkers. As a minimum it should include adhesive dressings, a roll of stretch adhesive, tape, moleskin, aspirin, tweezers and scissors.

Two items that you will hopefully not have to use are a torch (do not forget a spare battery), and a whistle to summon aid in case of an emergency. The recognised distress signal is six blasts of a whistle at ten-second intervals followed by a minute's silence, then six more blasts, and so on. The reply is three blasts at twenty-second intervals, repeated after a minute's pause.

You need not load yourself with an ice axe. It has already been mentioned that there will be no extensive snow and ice work on the walks in this book; although you may encounter the occasional patch, it will generally be well-trodden. Having said that, some walkers derive benefit from carrying a walking stick, and we have seen a few Continental trampers using ski sticks as walking aids.

One last tip: since no rucksack is completely waterproof, put your spare items of clothing in a plastic bag before packing them. Your food and your first aid kit should be in waterproof containers.

Food and Wine

Whether in a hotel or a mountain hut you will start the day with *Frühstück*, or breakfast. This will be a simple meal generally in Continental style, and rolls will be served with butter, jam, jelly, honey or marmalade and hot coffee and milk. Some hotels supply cooked meats and even cheese.

If you are out walking for the day you are quite likely to take a picnic lunch and once more bread rolls will be on your menu. To go with them you might select a local cheese from the many available, cooked meats or maybe pâté. Fruit, perhaps peaches, nectarines or grapes, makes a fine dessert. Alternatively, you may call at a mountain inn or hut for a midday meal. Have something light when you are walking; soup and a roll, perhaps. *Erbsensuppe* is a thick pea soup, *Gemüsesuppe*, vegetable soup, or you might take pot luck with *Tagesuppe* (soup of the day). You could try *Wurst*, sausages fried and served with bread and mustard, or perhaps an omelette or *Gulasch*.

By the time you get in after your walk you will certainly be ready for dinner, the main meal of the day. In an hotel this is usually of three or four courses, with a starter of soup or hors d'oeuvres. Some dishes you may come across are *Wiener Schnitzel* (veal cooked in batter), which, although Austrian, is very popular here; *Nudelfleisch* (noodles with chopped meat and gravy); *Kalbsbraten* (roast veal), and *Berner Platte*, a speciality of the Berne region which is a mixture of salt pork, boiled beef, sausages and pickled cabbage. Fish, especially trout, is another possibility. To go with any of these you may have *rosti*, a pan-fried potato dish, or noodles, known as *Teigwaren*. Cheese dishes such as fondue or raclette are world famous, and a delicious variation of the former is *Fondue Bourguignonne* in which cubes of steak replace the cubes of bread.

Switzerland is well known for its pastries and other desserts. *Obsttorten* (fruit tarts) and the wide range of gateaux available are delicious, while *Leckerli*,which is made from walnut marzipan, is justly popular. Fruit is frequently on the menu as a dessert, sometimes in the form of a *compote* (stewed).

French, Italian and German wines are, of course, obtainable, but since these can be expensive you should consider Swiss wines. Many come from the Rhône Valley and of these the red Dole is justifiably popular and often available *en carafe*. White wine is also made in this region and around Lake Geneva, while from Neuchâtel come light sparkling wines in red and white. More local wines are produced near the shores of Lake Thun, and of these the white Spiezer is among the best. The Swiss also make spirits and liqueurs from fruit. Kirsch, derived from cherries and their stones, is perhaps the best known of these, and others include Marc, Pfluemi and Williamine.

Below are a few useful names in German of some of the food and drinks you may encounter in the Bernese Oberland (in addition to those already mentioned):

Apple	*Apfel*	Crayfish	*Krebs*
Apple juice	*Apfelsaft*	Cream	*Rahm* or *Sahne*
Apricot	*Aprikose*	Cucumbers	*Gurken*
Asparagus	*Spargel*	Custard	*Pudding*
Bacon	*Speck*	Cutlet	*Kotelette*
Beans	*Bohnen*	Dessert	*Nachtisch*
Beef	*Rindfleisch*	Duck	*Ente*
Beef (roast)	*Rinderbraten*	Eel	*Aal*
Beer	*Bier*	Egg (fried)	*Spiegeleier*
Biscuit	*Keks*	Egg (scrambled)	*Ruhreier*
Bread	*Brot*	Figs	*Feigen*
Butter	*Butter*	Fish	*Fisch*
Cabbage	*Wiesskohl*	Game	*Wild*
Cake	*Kuchen*	Gin	*Wacholder*
Carrot	*Karotte*	Goose (roast)	*Gansebraten*
Cauliflower	*Blumenkohl*	Grapes	*Weintrauben*
Cheese	*Käse*	Gravy	*Sosse*
Cider	*Apfelmost* or *Most*	Haddock	*Schellfisch*
Cod	*Kabeljau*	Hake	*Hecht*

Halibut	*Heilbutt*
Ham	*Schinken*
Ham and eggs	*Eierspeise mit Schinken*
Ham (fried)	*Gerauchert Schinken*
Herring	*Hering*
Hock	*Rheinwein*
Honey	*Honig*
Hors d'oeuvre	*Vorspeise*
Ice cream	*Eis*
Jam	*Marmelade*
Kidney	*Niere*
Lamb	*Lammfleisch*
Leek	*Lauch*
Leg of deer	*Hirschschleger*
Lettuce	*Kopfsalat*
Liver sausage	*Leberwurst*
Lobster	*Hummer*
Marmalade	*Orangen Marmelade*
Meat	*Fleisch*
Meat dishes	*Fleischspeisen*
Meatloaf (baked)	*Hackbraten*
Melon	*Melone*
Menu	*Speisekarte*
Milk	*Milch*
Milk rice pudding	*Milchreiss*
Mushroom	*Pilze*
Mustard	*Seuf*
Nuts	*Nüsse*
Onion	*Zwiebel*
Orange	*Apfelsine*
Oysters	*Austern*
Paste	*Teig*
Peach	*Pfirsich*
Pear	*Birne*
Peas	*Erbsen*
Pepper	*Pfeffer*
Pie	*Pastete*
Pineapple	*Ananas*
Plum	*Pflaume*
Pork	*Schweinefleisch*
Pork (roast)	*Schweinsbraten*
Potato	*Kartoffel*
Potato (french fried)	*Backkartoffeln*
Poultry	*Geflügel*
Raspberry	*Himbeere*
Red wine	*Rotwein*
Rice	*Reis*
Saddle of venison	*Rehrücken*
Salt	*Salz*
Salmon	*Lachs*
Sandwich	*Belegte Brot*
Sardines in oil	*Olsardinen*
Sauce	*Sosse*
Shellfish	*Schalentiere*
Snails	*Schnecken*
Sole	*Scholle*
Soufflé	*Auflauf*
Soup (clear)	*Bouillon*
Spinach	*Spinat*
Steak	*Fleischschnitte* or *Beefsteak*
Strawberry	*Erdbette*
Sugar	*Zucker*
Sweet dishes	*Susspeisen* or *Mehlspeisen*
Tea	*Tee*
Tomato	*Tomate*
Tomato salad	*Tomatensalat*
Tongue	*Zunge*
Trout	*Forelle*
Truffles	*Truffeln*
Turkey	*Truthahn*
Turnip	*Rube*
Veal	*Kalbfleisch*
Veal cutlet	*Kalbschnitzel*
Veal (roast)	*Kalbsbraten*

Vegetable	*Gemüse*	White wine	*Weisswein*
Vinegar	*Essig*	Wine (a bottle of)	*Wein (eine Flasche)*
Walnut	*Walnuss*		
Water	*Wasser*		

Before you Go

No visas are necessary for Switzerland if you are a British Citizen, but you will need a passport.

There is no state medical health service in Switzerland, so insurance is a must and where you get it depends on how you are travelling. If you are motoring, you can get all-in insurance through the AA or RAC, and you will also need a Green Card from your motor insurers. Since you will certainly be travelling through at least one EEC country you should also apply, in good time, at your local Department of Health and Social Security for a Certificate of Entitlement E111. Information on how to obtain this is given on leaflet SA30. If you are camping or caravanning, the Carefree Insurance cover offered by the Camping and Caravanning Club is extremely competitive. If you are flying or going by train and booking through a travel agent, you can arrange insurance at the same time. Package holidays usually include comprehensive holiday insurance.

Motorists have other arrangements to make apart from insurance. As already mentioned, there is a Motorway Tax in Switzerland. If you want to use the Swiss motorways you need to display a *vignette*, which is obtainable from the AA or RAC for £11 (double if you have a caravan or trailer). The *vignette* is valid during the year of issue and up to 31 January of the subsequent year, and failure to show it while driving on a motorway could mean a hefty fine.

The other items for the motorist to negotiate are the ferry tickets. These should be applied for as early as possible and can be obtained through motoring organisations. You could consider purchasing shares in a shipping company to qualify for concessionary fares. If you contemplate taking your vehicle by ferry several times over the course of a few years, this is certainly a viable proposition. Ownership of £600 worth of P&O's 5.5 per cent Redeemable Non-Cumulative Preferred Stock qualifies you for 50 per cent discount on the Dover routes and 40 per cent discount for voyages from Portsmouth. For investments of between £300 and £599 discounts are 25 per cent and 20 per cent respectively. Reductions apply to standard rates for private vehicles and accompanying passengers, not for foot passengers, sleeping accommodation, towed caravans and trailers, or special fares. Since there is no limit to the number of concessionary trips in a year, you could see an appreciable return on your investment within a reasonable time and in the meantime also receive the dividend. Application for voyages subject to concessions have to be made to P&O Concessionary Fare Department.

If you decide to purchase a Swiss Pass, a Swiss Card or a Swiss Half Fare Travel Card (*see under* 'Getting About'), you must do so before travelling to Switzerland. The same applies to a Rail Europe Senior Card (*see under* 'How to Get There').

You may want to purchase your maps before you leave for your holiday (*see under* 'How the Walks are Organised').

There is one other preparation you can make for your holiday. Make sure you are walking fit. Two or three long walks in the fortnight before you depart will help you enjoy your holiday that much more.

Hazards

If there is any country where the visitor is unlikely to catch some dread disease, Switzerland is it. In the mountains everything seems to be healthily clean, and the air is as pure as you could wish. The only disease you must be wary of is rabies, and that's a hazard almost everywhere except the British Isles. Be on your guard if you see any animal that appears ill or aggressive. If you get bitten seek medical advice at the earliest possible moment. Having said that, we have never heard of anyone catching rabies in the Swiss Alps.

Water is sometimes treated with suspicion. In the mountains it should be pure enough, although where animals are grazing on nearby slopes it is prudent not to take water from a stream. You will frequently pass wooden troughs fed by continuously flowing pipes. This crystal clear liquid seems to be safe and we have come to no harm yet.

Now that there are no bears left in the Oberland, the only dangerous animals (apart from rabid ones) are poisonous snakes. Adders do exist in the Alps but they are comparatively rare. It is unusual for anyone to be bitten and bites are rarely fatal. Keep your eyes open in wild country by all means, but the chances of even seeing a snake are low.

Walking is not, or should not be a hazardous activity, nevertheless, in wild mountain country there are certain risks of which the visitor must be aware. In the walk descriptions it is indicated which routes are more difficult or more exposed than others, but it is up to each individual to assess his or her capabilities, or those of the party. Remember that inclement weather can make any route more difficult or dangerous, especially rain or mist. Snow is possible down to 2,000m (6,500ft), even in summer, and a sudden shower could transform a rough mountain path. Never put off the decision to turn back if conditions dictate.

One weather effect that can be frightening when you are high on a mountain is a thunderstorm. Although a fatal lightning strike is quite rare, there are certain precautions you should take when a thunderstorm is imminent. Never remain on high points or exposed ridges. Get away from wire fences or safety cables. Do not shelter under overhanging rocks; this is the classic spark gap situation. Keep away from isolated trees and single buildings. If you are in a flat exposed area, sit down, pull your legs up to your chin and clasp your hands around your legs. The object of this is to keep the area of contact with the ground as small as possible – it has been suggested that the ideal attitude is to squat with the heels off the ground. How long you would maintain this is debatable...

Another hazard might be heatstroke. The summer sun in the Alps can be quite powerful and carrying a water bottle and wearing a sun-hat, preferably wide-brimmed, are precautions that you can take. At the other extreme, frostbite might cause problems. If you go walking in the Oberland during the approved months (May to September), and keep off the higher routes when snow and ice are present, frostbite is not very likely. Still, do carry extra warm clothing and, in case of a disabling accident, a bivvy-bag.

There is no real danger of avalanches during the walking season, but there are places where you could be hit by falling rocks. Stones can be dislodged by animals or other walkers so be careful where you sit down for lunch. Watch out for signs; they usually bear the approved graphic warning, but may carry the word '*Steinschlag*' on them.

In the unlikely event of an accident remember the universal distress signals of six blasts of a whistle at ten-second intervals followed by a minute's silence, then six more blasts, and so on. Instead of whistle blasts you can use light flashes. The reply to the distress signal is three blasts or flashes at twenty-second intervals, repeated after a minute's pause.

If you are anywhere near an SAC hut, they have radio telephones.

The People and the Country

Until comparatively recently, in historical terms, Switzerland was a relatively poor country, but in modern times an abundance of cheap hydroelectric power combined with the industry and thrift of the Swiss people, has changed all that. Switzerland now has one of the most stable economies in the western world, and its outstanding record of low inflation bears this out. The country aims to be as self sufficient in food production as it possibly can, and their system was seen to be most successful during the war. As you walk in the mountains you will see how well they use land that seems almost impossible to farm. In summer they take their animals up to the high pastureland, and elsewhere practically every available plot of grass is mown for winter fodder, sometimes three times during the summer months. To maintain the necessary workforce, the Swiss Government pay substantial subsidies to mountain farmers. This has arrested the movement of workers from agriculture to the industrial cities. In the Oberland you will see much evidence of high-altitude farming. Small one-family summer farms are here and there, such as at Fisialp above Kandersteg, Brechalp above the Lauterbrunnental or at Oberbärgli, on the Hohtürli path. Some farms are bigger, communal affairs. Small villages abound, like Selden in the Gasteretal, Gimmel near Mürren or Saxeten above Wilderswil.

Tourism is now a major industry and has transformed many villages that formerly depended on agriculture for their survival.

From their history and traditions it follows that the Swiss are hard-working but friendly people, and you will almost always find them courteous and helpful. They are also, by and large, a clean and tidy race. Those used to seeing litter-strewn streets and roadsides in Britain will find the contrast with Swiss towns and countryside striking. The Swiss are generally active in their leisure time. Tennis and golf are popular, and many indulge in sailing, particularly on Lakes Brienz and Thun. Paragliding has become one of the most noticeable pastimes, and on a fine day there are usually a few brightly-coloured parachutes adorning the landscape near to popular resorts. These devotees seem to get up to the most improbable places from which to launch themselves into space.

The most practised leisure activity, however, is walking. Swiss people walk because they like exercise and because they love their mountains. Some of the more popular routes have a continuous stream of walkers on them and a high proportion are walking in their own country. The extremes in the shape and age of those tramping the trails are remarkable – thin and fat, short and tall, some are in their seventies and eighties, some quite young children walking with the family. While we were out on Walk 2 following one of the thinnest of *Bergwegs* across the exposed face of Gsür, we encountered two youngsters no older than five or six roped on a length of line to their parents. We would not recommend this walk for children, but obviously some have no such qualms.

Switzerland has four official languages – German, French, Italian and Romansch. About two-thirds of the population speak German, and that is the language spoken in the Bernese Oberland. Whereas High German is used for books, teaching and all formal occasions, the German spoken in everyday use is slightly different. This is no drawback because many people, particularly those connected with tourism, speak English. However, a few words of German are useful:

English	German
Good-morning	*Guten Morgen*
Good-afternoon	*Guten Tag*
Good-evening	*Guten Abend*
Good-night	*Gute Nacht*
Goodbye	*Auf Wiedersehen*
Yes	*Ja*
No	*Nein*
Thank you	*Danke*
Please	*Bitte*
You're welcome	*Bitte*
Excuse me (I didn't hear)	*Wiebitte*
Excuse me (may I get past)	*Gestatten Sie*

Notices

English	German
Caution	*Achtung*
Lift	*Aufzug*
Exit	*Ausgang*
Information	*Auskunft*
Occupied	*Besetzt*
Entrance	*Eingang*
Free (or Vacant)	*Frei*
Danger	*Gefahr*
Closed	*Geschlossen*
Cashiers	*Kasse*
Danger of Death	*Lebensgefahr*
No Smoking	*Nichtraucher* or *Rauchen Verboten*
Reserved	*Reserviert*
Pull	*Ziehen*

While out walking you may be greeted in a variety of languages, but the most used greeting will be *Gruezi*, which sounds like '*Grootsee*'. Most people that you meet will be friendly and eager to communicate.

Further Information

Emergency Services

The emergency services may be summoned by ringing the following numbers: 117 for the Police, 118 for the Fire Brigade, 144 for the Ambulance. Other useful telephone numbers are: 143, 'The Helping Hand', 162, the weather forecast and 163, road conditions. These announcements will be in German.

Post and Telephone Services

Letter boxes in Switzerland are painted yellow. Post offices are numerous and open at 7.30 am, with closing time Mondays to Fridays 6.15 or 6.30 pm, and lunch break from 12 noon to 1.45 pm. Saturday closing is 11am or 12 noon, but can be later in larger towns. Postcards to European countries outside Switzerland need a SFr 0.80 stamp. Letters up to 20g need a SFr 0.90 stamp for Western European countries. Correspondence can be forwarded to Swiss post offices for collection. All envelopes must be addressed to the person who will collect it, Poste restante, with the name of the town preceded by the postcode. The sender's address should be marked on the back. All unclaimed mail is returned to the sender if not collected within 30 days. On collection, the addressee is expected to produce his or her passport for identification.

To make a call to the UK from a public telephone box, lift the receiver, insert coins to the amount displayed on the apparatus and check for the dial tone (may be different from the UK dial tone). Dial 00 44 followed by the STD code, leaving out the first 0, then dial the telephone number. Wait a few seconds (there may be unfamiliar tones during this time) before getting a ringing or engaged tone. A persistent tone or recorded announcement means that your call has not got through. Hang up and try again. Watch the display to see when to insert other coins.

Medical Facilities

There is a well-equipped hospital in Interlaken and doctors and dentists are in residence in the resort villages. Switzerland has no reciprocal health arrangement with the UK, so medical treatment has to be paid for in full. You can claim on your insurance afterwards.

Electricity

The supply in Switzerland is 220 volts a.c. Plug sockets are for Continental plugs, so if you are taking electrical appliances you will need to pack an adaptor.

Tourist Offices

You will find a tourist office in every town and village of reasonable size in the Bernese Oberland. In them you can obtain general information and a variety of leaflets, including hotel lists, apartment lists and timetables, and you can also buy maps, books and posters. In addition, tourist offices will assist in finding and reserving hotel accommodation, and they also act as lost property offices.

National Holidays

In Switzerland national holidays are on New Year's Day, Good Friday, Easter Monday, Ascension Day, Whit Monday, National Day (1 August), Christmas Day and 26 December. National Day is really Swiss Independence Day, and is celebrated by staging processions, bonfires and firework displays. Many hotels put on special meals; if you intend to reserve a table on 1 August, do book early.

Religion

Protestant and Catholic churches are found in most places. Services in English are held at times in the Protestant Church (Reformierte Kirche) at Kandersteg, the Schlosskirche in Interlaken and in the English Churches at Adelboden, Mürren, Wengen and Grindelwald.

Tourist Tax

This is added to all bills for accommodation. For everyone over 16 years of age staying at hotels, pensions and apartments it is SFr 1.60 each and in youth hostels, tents, caravans, holiday centres and group accommodation it is SFr 1. Children from 6 to 16 pay half and younger children do not pay at all.

In return, every taxpayer receives a Visitor's Card which can be used to obtain reductions when visiting museums, castles and certain concerts. In some resorts it also allows reductions in some sports facilities.

Embassies and Consulates

Embassy of Great Britain
Thunstrasse 50
CH-3005 Berne

Tel: 031 44 50 21

Embassy of Eire
Eigerstrasse 71
CH-3007 Berne

Tel: 031 46 23 53

Consulate General of Great Britain
Dufourstrasse 56
CH-8008 Zurich

Tel: 01 47 15 20

Other Useful Addresses

Swiss National Tourist Office
Swiss Centre
New Coventry Street
London W1V 8EE

Tel: 071 734 1921
Fax: 071 437 4577
Telex: 21295

(The official representative of the Swiss Federal Railways can be found at the same address.)

Youth Hostels Association (YHA)
(England and Wales)
Trevelyan House
8 St Stephen's Hill
St Albans
Herts

Tel: 0727 45057

Schweizerischer Bund für
Jugendherbergen (SBJ)
(Swiss Youth Hostels)
Engestrasse 9
CH-3012 Berne 22

Tel: 031 24 55 03

Camping and Caravanning Club Ltd
Greenfields House
Westwood Way
Coventry CV4 8JH

Tel no: 0203 694995

Schweizerischer Camping und
Caravanning Verband (SCCV)
(Swiss Camping and Caravanning
Federation)
Habsburgerstrasse 35
CH-6004 Lucerne

Tel: 040 23 48 22

Verband Schweizer Campings (VSC)
(Swiss Camping Association)
Im Sydefadeli 40
CH-8037 Zurich

Tel: 01 44 57 13

THE WALKS

Walk 1 Adelboden – Engstligen Falls – Engstligenalp – Ärtelen – Laueli – Adelboden

Map nos:	Adelboden Wanderkarte (1:25,000) Swiss Survey 263 (1:50,000), 1247 & 1267 (1:25,000)
Walking time:	6 hours 45 minutes
Grading:	Strenuous. The first section of the route including the *Geissweg* has no real exposure, but there is moderate exposure on the Ärtelen section.
Highest altitude:	*Bergweg* above Ärtelen 2,047m (6,716ft)
Lowest altitude:	Schutzen Bridge 1,238m (4,062ft)

The valley to the south of Adelboden is closed at its head, about three miles from the town, by a wall of rock. Beyond the top of the wall is the Engstligenalp, one of the most remarkable features in the Alps, a square, flat-bottomed arena. The waters collected in this huge dish plunge over the precipice as the Engstligen Falls then flow down the valley as the Engstligenbach.

This walk is first along the bank of this river to the bottom of the falls, which are among the most magnificent in Switzerland. The route then goes up the cliff by way of a path known as the *Geissweg* (Goats' Way) and enters the Engstligenalp. The return is by way of a narrow mountain path through the Ärtelen area, then along the eastern flank of the valley to Laueli, finally descending to the river and climbing again to Adelboden.

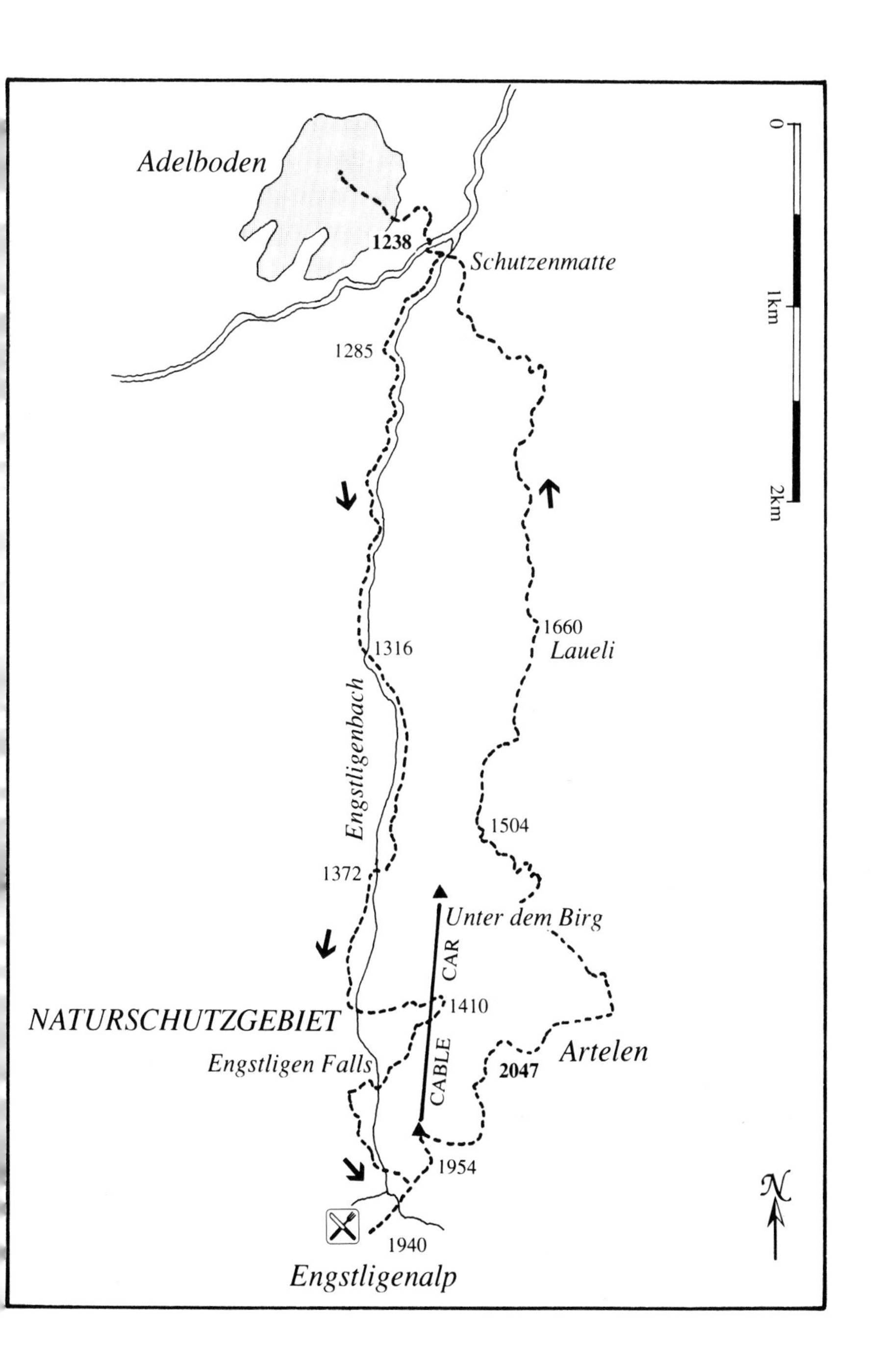
Adelboden
1238
Schutzenmatte
1285
1316
1660
Laueli
Engstligenbach
1504
1372
Unter dem Birg
CABLE CAR
NATURSCHUTZGEBIET
1410
Artelen
Engstligen Falls
2047
1954
1940
Engstligenalp
0
1km
2km
N

The Walk

From the bus station, walk south for a short distance then turn left down a path just before the Sport Hotel Adler. Go straight over a minor road then over a section of main road on to another path. At the bottom go straight over another part of the main road and down a minor road to cross the Schutzen Bridge. Bear left along the Bunderlenstrasse to a sawmill on the right and turn right to walk along the side of the Engstligenbach, occasionally getting a glimpse of the waterfall at the head of the valley. Keep to the right-hand side of the river, ignoring all turn-offs, until you reach an attractive covered footbridge.

Cross the footbridge and bear right along a road for a short distance, then, where the road goes right over a bridge, keep straight on along a track. Shortly, the track climbs away from the river and you see the falls ahead, now looking much more imposing. The path crosses two rock-strewn gullies, before ending at a road. Turn right for 100m, crossing the river then turning left on a path that goes up the west bank of the Engstligenbach. The lower section of the falls is in constant view now, and appearing to grow taller by the minute. Just below the fall the path goes left, over a bridge. At a fork, on the other side, bear right on a *Bergweg*, through a wooded area. The path climbs through the trees and has already gained some height by the time it joins the main route from Unter dem Birg, known as the *Geissweg* (Goats' Way). Turn right up this wider, well-engineered path that winds its way upward. Although there are vertical drops to the side in places, it is quite safe, with safety cables in place if required.

At a junction go right, towards the upper fall. Clouds of spray fill the air as you cross a footbridge just below the thundering cascade – you can get wet here! Climb up the other side and, after the path levels out, go on to cross another footbridge. Proceed to a T-junction at the edge of the Engstligenalp and turn right to the Berghaus Bartschi (restaurant and refreshments).

Between this position and the slopes of the Wildstrubel is a vast area of pastureland with a sizeable population of cattle. There are chalets here and there and dairy produce may be purchased at some of them. Mountains almost surround the Alp. To the east, a ridge that comes from the Gross Lohner rises over the peculiar rock peaks of the Tschingellochtighorn, the Chindbettihorn and the Tierhörnli. The south wall is one of dazzling white, being the snowy slopes of the Steghorn and the Wildstrubel, while to the south-west the Ammertengrat falls from the Wildstrubel to the Ammerten Pass. The north-western aspect is closed in by the massif that includes the Rotstock and the Fitzer. You can wander at will on the Alp and it is not proposed to suggest any route here.

Approaching Engstligenalp

To return, go back past the T-junction that you came in on and approach the Berg Hotel (restaurant and refreshments, including a self-service section). Opposite this building turn right on a *Bergweg* that climbs towards the rim of the Alp at its north-eastern corner. Beyond, it enters the region of Ärtelen and undulates as it crosses a number of streams. After passing the Ärtelenbach the path climbs to where a track to the Lohnerhutte goes off to the right. Here the route passes through a rotary stile and then begins to descend with a degree of exposure to the left. The surface is loose and unpleasant and the slopes below are steep indeed. Gradually, the sense of exposure lessens and the path embarks on a descending traverse from which there is a different view of the Engstligen Falls.

Eventually the path takes a more direct line downwards, descending in a series of small hairpins, to a junction of tracks. Turn right on a *Bergweg* that proceeds along the flank of the valley in a series of ascents and descents, though rather more up than down. When you see a chalet up to the right you will be near the high point of the path. This now becomes a paved way of vehicular width and, after little more than a quarter-mile of this (just after passing a barn), go left on a *Bergweg*.

Go to the right of a barn in a sloping field, under the cables of a ski-lift and through a belt of trees, before emerging on to a road near a hairpin bend. Walk down the road in the same line for perhaps 200m, then go left on a path signposted 'Boden' (the Stubli Restaurant is only 100m further down the road). Go past a chalet and down to a junction, where you turn right.

The path is narrow at first, but widens as it traverses a number of fields, emerging on to a road by a barn. Turn right and immediately left on a path that goes through a gap in a fence and soon bends right. Pass to the right of another barn, through a gap in a fence and walk towards another chalet. Go to the left of the building and descend a narrow path to emerge on to a road by the bridge over the Engstligenbach.

Cross the bridge and reverse the first part of the route, back to the bus station.

There is a cableway at the head of the valley that plies up and down from the Engstligenalp. To reach the bottom station turn left on the road at the valley head instead of going right. Use of the cable car would reduce walking time by $1^1/_2$–$1^3/_4$ hours.

Walk 2 Adelboden – Schwandfälspitz – Furggialp – Hornbruck – Gilbach – Adelboden

Map nos:	Adelboden Wanderkarte (1:25,000) Swiss Survey 263 (1:50,000), 1247 (1:25,000)
Walking time:	6 hours 45 minutes
Grading:	Strenuous. Moderate exposure on some parts of the Gsür traverse.
Highest altitude:	South face of Gsür 2,200m (7,218ft)
Lowest altitude:	Allebach bridge 1,297m (4,255ft)

Gsür is a rocky summit to the north-west of Adelboden; its south-east ridge comes down to the secondary peak of the Schwandfälspitz. The walk ascends to the Schwandfälspitz from Adelboden then up the lower part of Gsür's south-east ridge. It then branches left to traverse the south face of Gsür and descends to Furggialp. The route then goes down to and across the Allebach and over to the Gilbach before returning to Adelboden.

The walk can be shortened by about two hours by taking the chairlift from Adelboden to near the top of the Schwandfälspitz (one-way fare SFr 5.40, with 26 per cent discount to Half Fare Travel Card holders).

The Walk

From Adelboden's bus station walk along the Dorfstrasse and turn right into the Senggistrasse. After clearing the town's buildings the broad track climbs onwards up the mountainside by means of a series of long sweeping hairpins, mostly through woodland. The final sweep ends by the top chairlift station where there is a restaurant (refreshments). Go left and climb the final metres to the summit of the Schwandfälspitz at 2,027m (6,650ft).

There is another restaurant to the west of the peak which is a fine viewpoint, with many of the Oberland giants visible. The Eiger, the Mönch and the Jungfrau just show above the intervening mountains to the east, and to the right of them are the Blümlisalp and the Doldenhorn with the lower Fründenhorn between. The local peaks to the south-east and south are

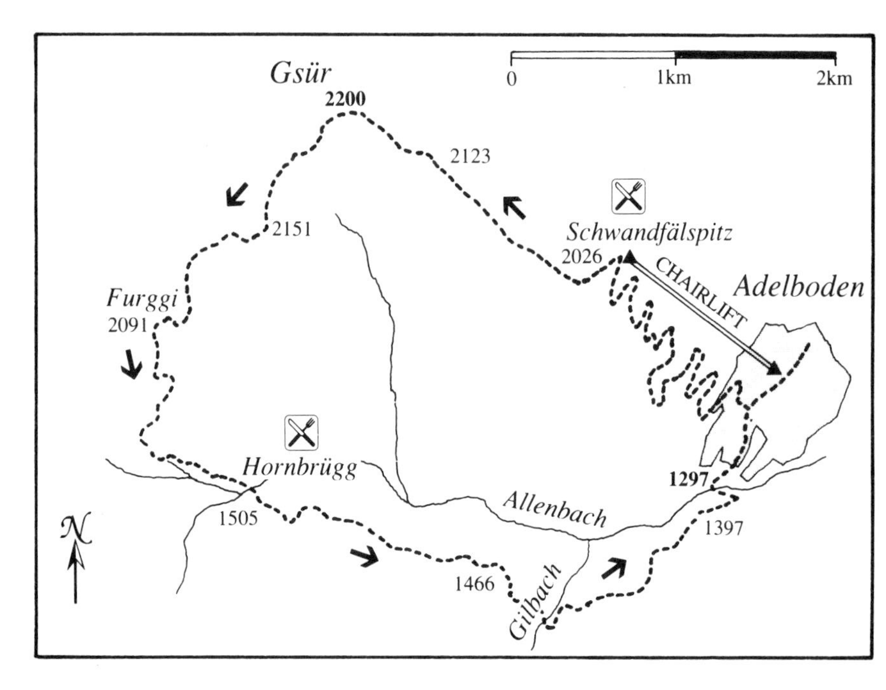

all included in the panorama – the rocky Lohners, the abrupt Tschingellochtighorn, then the Chindbettihorn, Tierhörnli, the Steghorn and the flat-topped white mass of the Wildstrubel, in that order. To the right of them are more summits, with the snowy Wildhorn the most prominent. Looking north, a series of rocky peaks range between Gsür and the Niesen, and to the right of them are the Sigriswilgrat and the Niederhorn, both on the other side of Lake Thun. Pilatus, near Lake Lucerne can also be seen.

Leaving the summit, go through a gate and follow the ridge towards the peak of Gsür. In under 0.8km, cross a ladder stile and take the narrow path that edges left away from the ridge to start the high route across the south face of Gsür.

This is a somewhat complex face with numerous gullies breaking it into a series of buttresses, so that the route is far from straight. From afar the path is not easy to see and the terrain has an impressive look to it. Like many other similar mountain tracks it looks much more difficult than it is. The slopes to the left are steep although at first there is not much sense of exposure. However, the path is quite narrow and in places almost non-existent. Further across the face there are situations that could be described as exposed and at one place there is a short scramble from one level to another.

Having completed the traverse you now descend towards the chalet of

Furggi, passing to the left of the building and going straight on at a junction of paths. Now, descend the vast mountainside towards the Allebach – the path is steep in places and has become eroded by water action. (Among the many wild flowers on the lower slopes you may see the purple gentian, a rather large plant that is surprisingly part of the same family as the tiny snow gentian. Near the bottom, the path goes past a pleasant picnic site and just below is a bridge over the Allebach. This river has brought down vast quantities of debris from the slopes of the Albristhorn and the result is rather unsightly. There is evidence that the authorities are trying to tidy it up, but shifting even a small portion of these piles of rubble will be a mammoth task.

Cross the bridge and walk up the road on the other side. Turn left and shortly come to the Restaurant Aebi (refreshments). Follow the road over to the Gilbach valley and at a T-junction by the Hotel des Alpes, turn left for a short distance. Turn right on a path by a private garage (house named Krambarnbuli) and cross a field. Go down a flight of steps to cross the Gilbach. Turn left on the other side and and walk through bushes, then up a bank to a rotary stile. On reaching a road, go left along it and after a quarter-mile bear left. In another half-mile turn sharply left and walk down to the Allebach. Cross the stone bridge, go up the road to Adelboden and turn right at the top into the Dorfstrasse to walk along to the bus station.

Walk 3 Adelboden – Allebach – Scharmtanne – Daubenfels – Adelboden

Map nos:	Adelboden Wanderkarte (1:25,000) Swiss Survey 263 (1:50,000), 1247 (1:25,000).
Walking time:	3 hours
Grading:	Easy. No exposure anywhere.
Highest altitude:	Fluhweide 1,610m (5,282ft).
Lowest altitude:	Allebach bridge 1,297m (4,255ft)

The Allebach flows from the mountains to the west of Adelboden and comes down a west/east valley to pass to the south of the town before joining the Engstligenbach.

This walk is first along the south bank of the Allebach, then follows the Stigelbach to the Scharmtanne restaurant. A pleasant return route contours the northern flank of the valley to the Schwandfälspitz path, then rises past the viewpoint at Daubenfels before descending to Adelboden.

The Walk

Since there is no railway station in Adelboden, the route begins at the bus station, situated at the north end of the town.

Walk down the main street (Dorfstrasse) and turn left down the Risetenstrassli (opposite the Haus Sunnegold). Follow it down to the Allebach stream and cross the stone bridge. Immediately turn right to walk along the side of the river. Keep to the left of the stream and presently pass under a modern bridge supported on high piers. The path has been mostly through trees, but soon it moves away from the river to emerge into the open before teeing into another path. Turn right and walk with the peak of the Albristhorn in front, and that of Gsür a little to the right. The path edges nearer the river again, passing a picnic site with a wooden shelter.

Turn right over a long wooden bridge, stopping to look back downstream and admire the rugged Lohner group of mountains to the right of the valley. The Stigelbach joins the Allebach just above the bridge and the route now

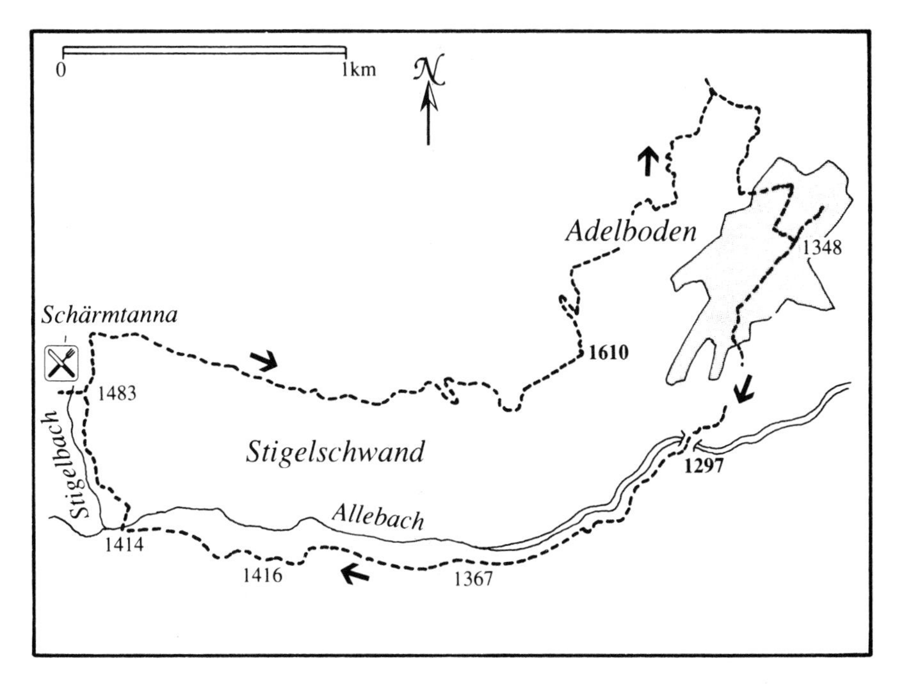

goes up the east side of this stream. Coming to a road, go left to the bridge. The stream is not an object of beauty – like the Allebach, the Stigelbach has brought down a huge amount of rubble, creating a wide unsightly bed – but the backing mountain scenery is magnificent.

Just a few yards further along from the bridge is the Scharmtanne restaurant (refreshments).

Return to the east side of the Stigelbach and continue to follow it, but after a short distance turn right and walk along a narrow path that contours the hillside. The views to the right are compelling; if you prefer to keep your eyes on the path while walking, there are many seats along the way where you can sit and enjoy the scenery. The Wildstrubel is partly hidden by the nearer Fitzer and Rotstock. To the left of it are the Steghorn, Tierhörnli, the Chindbettihorn, then the distinctive shape of the Tschingellochtighorn, looking rather like a fortress. Further left still is the rugged mass of the Grosse Lohner.

The path has, thus far, been along the bottom edge of woodland. Now, at one point it enters a wooded area where it crosses a stream and goes up some steps to emerge on to open hillside. Climbing round two hairpin bends, the path levels, then, after passing a chalet, drops slightly to join the wider Schwandfälspitz path. Turn right to descend it. Go round a left-hand bend

Above the Allebach Valley

Kleine and Grosse Lohner from Daubenfels

and on to the next right-hand hairpin. Turn left and climb between pine trees to the viewpoint of Daubenfels.

The mass of the Grosse Lohner is now almost opposite and you can appreciate its ruggedness. There are several individual summits – from right to left, the Vorder Lohner, the Mittlere Lohner, the Hindere Lohner and the Kleine Lohner. Between the last two is the distinctive gap of the Bunderchrinde. Further to the left are the summits of the Bunderspitz, First and Stand.

From the viewpoint walk on up the rising path then bear right on a *Bergweg*. Descend to a chalet where the path bends right, later becoming a veritable staircase of steps. Go down between attractive chalets until the path becomes a road. Follow this down past the church to Adelboden's Dorfstrasse. To return to the bus station, turn left.

Walk 4 Kandersteg – Oeschinensee – Kandersteg

Map nos:	Kandersteg Wanderkarte (1:25,000) Swiss Survey 263 & 264 (1:50,000), 1247 & 1248 (1:25,000)
Walking time:	2 hours 45 minutes
Grading:	Moderate. No real exposure anywhere.
Highest altitude:	Above Oeschinensee 1,675m (5,495ft)
Lowest altitude:	Kandersteg 1,175m (3,855ft)

Barely 3km east of Kandersteg, and 400 metres higher, lies the beautiful lake of Oeschinensee. It is situated in a natural bowl, surrounded by spectacular mountains, some of which rise from the shore. This is a spot to sit and contemplate the magnificent scenery, sip a cool drink, eat a typically Swiss meal or go rowing on the lake's blue waters.

The walk ascends along the north side of the Öschibach stream and returns generally down the line of the chairlift. The route described is suitable for any member of the family who can walk, and it is possible to cut it short by riding down on the chairlift (SFr 6.60, only 16 per cent reduction for Half Fare Travel Card holders). You can also ride up and walk down.

The Walk

From Kandersteg railway station walk up to the main street and turn left. After a short distance you will see the information centre on the right. Immediately beyond, cross the Öschibach stream and turn right. Walk with the stream to your right, soon passing a diminutive, picturesque church. The mountains that can be seen ahead up the valley are the Rothorn and the Blümlisalphorn. Where the Rendezvous Campsite is signposted to the left, keep straight on and climb steadily until the LWK station is reached. Just beyond the buildings take a narrow, rougher path to the left. The gradient increases and the path winds in places until it levels out.

Soon you come to a T-junction, where you go left on a tarmac surface. Although this section is used by vehicles it is extremely steep and remains so

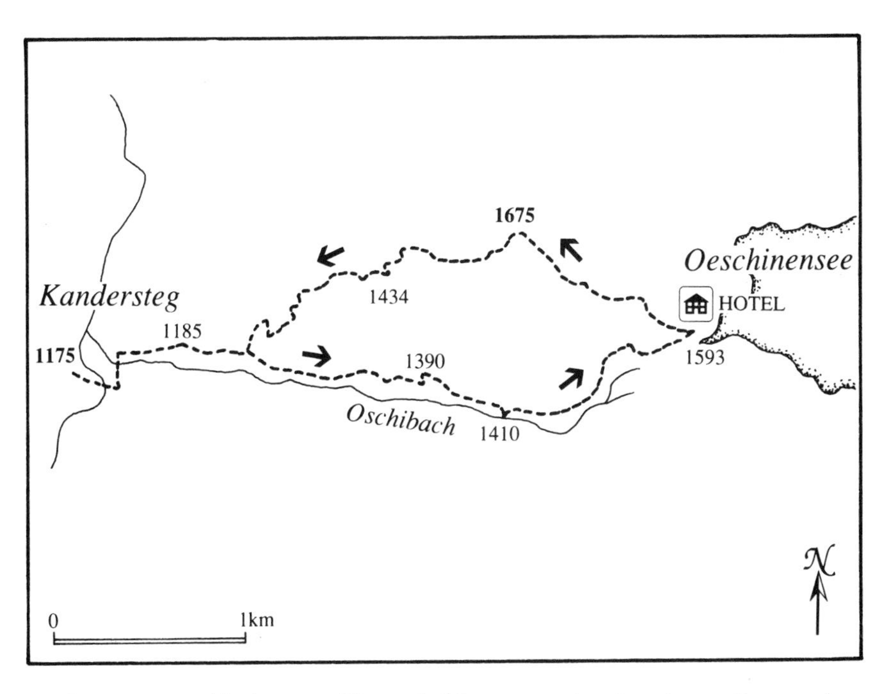

for an appreciable distance. The end of the tarmac signals easier gradients and the route, previously through trees, is now in more open ground. Rounding a bend brings the Oeschinensee (altitude 1,522m, 4,993ft) into view, with its dramatic backdrop of mountains. Oval in shape and a little over a mile long, it owes its colouring to the glacier water that constantly feeds into it. The peaks in view are, from left to right, the Rothorn, the Blümlisalphorn, the Oeschinenhorn and the Fründenhorn. On the skyline, to the left of the Rothorn, the Blümlisalp Hutte can be made out. This is a Swiss Alpine Club hut just above the Hohtürli Pass. Closer at hand, as you advance along the path above the lake, are the Hotel Oeschinensee and the Berghaus Oeschinensee, each with a restaurant. Accommodation, if required, is available at either place or at the Berghaus Lager.

For the return, take the path signposted 'Sesselbahn' that climbs through woodland then levels out as open ground is reached. If you go straight on at a four-way junction you will reach the chairlift station in five minutes; if you prefer to walk down, turn left. After about 150m bear right on a path that is none too distinct (do not follow the straight-on trail which is more prominent but leads nowhere). The path climbs again slightly then enters a wood through a gap in a wire fence. It soon re-emerges into the open and the chairlift can be seen ahead. By a hut, just short of the cables, go left down a

Boats for hire on the Oeschinensee

The church at Kandersteg

slope. Cross a wall with the help of a short ladder and commence a zigzag section. Take care here, for the ground is steep.

A little lower, the route passes a hut where cheese is made and can be bought. The path then swings right, across the slope and through a narrow gate. Another gate gives access to a belt of trees and soon the chairlift is again reached.

The path now zigzags down the line of the chairlift with the Rendezvous Campsite in view below. Eventually the path bears left and goes down through the campsite. Take the exit road and at the first junction turn right and retrace your steps to the starting point of the walk.

Walk 5 Selden – Kanderfirn – Selden – Eggeschwand

Map nos:	Kandersteg Wanderkarte (1:25,000) Swiss Survey 263 & 264 (1:50,000), 1247, 1267 & 1268 (1:25,000)
Walking time:	6 hours 15 minutes
Grading:	Strenuous. Part of the ascent to the Kanderfirn is a little exposed.
Highest altitude:	Above Kanderfirn 2,411m (7,910ft)
Lowest altitude:	Eggeschwand 1,194m (3,917ft)

The Gasteretal is one of the most spectacular valleys in the Alps, and the height and steepness of its sides are almost without parallel. It lies to the south-east of Kandersteg and the only means of access for vehicles is a narrow, rough road. Motorists can gain access on payment of a hefty toll, but it is also possible to travel up to the hamlet of Selden by minibus. This service is operated by Taxi Schmid of Frutigen (033 71 11 71 or 033 75 16 26) and leaves Kandersteg railway station at 7.30am, 9.30am and 10.40am. Would-be passengers are advised to be there early if they haven't booked in advance. Although the proprietors do their best to please everyone, there must occasionally be disappointments. The single fare is SFr 8 – not outrageously high when you consider the wear and tear on vehicles and the skill and nerve of the drivers. It also compares very favourably with cableway fares.

The entrance to the Gasteretal is gained by a steep and twisty road of indifferent surface. There are two short tunnels and the bus emerges to cross the river Kander as it tumbles through the narrow Chluse Gorge. Selden is 6.5km up the valley and from here the walk goes on along the north side of the river Kander, transferring later to the south flank for the climb to the Kanderfirn. The return is back down the same route but staying south of the river until Selden. The walk down to Eggeschwand is constantly changing from one river bank to the other and includes the exciting Chluse Gorge.

From Eggeschwand there is a bus service to Kandersteg (SFr 1.5), but if you prefer to walk, add 25 minutes to the time.

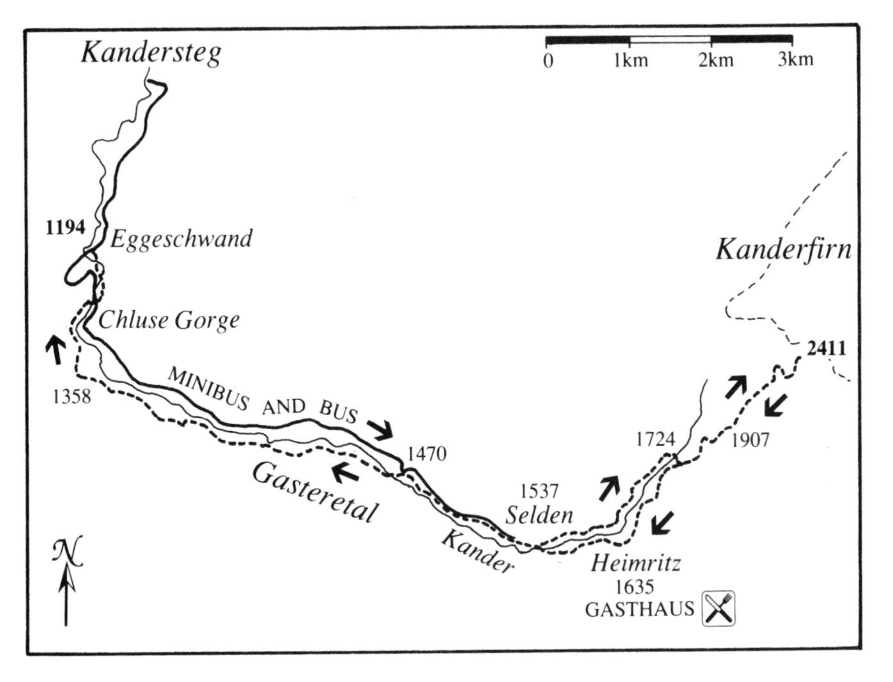

The Walk

Having disembarked from the minibus outside the Hotel Gasteretal in Selden, walk on up the track, which remains wide enough for a vehicle as far as the Gasthaus Heimritz (refreshments), reached in 20 minutes. Here, bear left off the vehicular track and follow a path that is still comfortably wide. Eventually it narrows and becomes a typical *Bergweg*, crossing a series of avalanche gullies before descending to the river near a bridge.

Cross the bridge and go left on a path that climbs away from the river. The snout of the Kanderfirn Glacier has been in sight at the head of the valley for most of the walk, and the majestic waterfall that drops from the left-hand side has been a feature of the landscape. Other wispy falls decorate the rock wall below the mass of ice. Cows graze on the grassy slopes, where harebells of several types, pinks, houseleeks, white and yellow daisies and minute snow gentians are just a few of the species growing.

The path crosses several streams then climbs to gain the crest of an ancient glacier moraine. It follows this crest for some distance with long, steep slopes to the left hand. However, the path is so wide that there is little sense of exposure. The moraine eventually merges with the mountainside and the path zigzags steeply on, passing through a belt where the *Alpenrose* grows in

Looking towards the Kanderfin Glacier

some profusion. Eventually a buttress is rounded and after a little more climbing the glacier appears below. A path continues to and on to the glacier, but unless you have the necessary experience and equipment you are advised not to venture on to it.

Return down the same route as far as the bridge, but, instead of re-crossing it, keep down the left bank of the river. Not too well defined in places, the path crosses several streams but remains in open ground until a ladder stile gives access to a wood. It descends to the water's edge, then goes past a bridge to Heimritz. Stay on the left bank until the next bridge which is just above Selden. There are two hotels here, the Gasteretal and the Steinbok, and you may decide to stop at one or the other for some refreshment. You could cut the walk short here and return by minibus, if there is room; had you planned to do this, a return ticket would have been SFr 13.

To continue the walk, proceed down the road for about half a mile then bear left by two seats, down a well-engineered path between trees. This path eventually zigzags down to the river by a bridge. Cross the bridge and bear round right on a track of vehicular width. In about a mile re-cross the river and after a few yards turn left on a footpath through trees. At a junction turn sharply left and cross the river by means of a two-part bridge, then go right on a path through trees. After crossing a secondary stream the path veers

Mountain goats in the Gasteretal

leftward to a junction where there are some seats. You cannot help but admire the fine waterfall that drops down the south side of the valley, perhaps the best one along this route, but there are more to come.

Turning right at the junction, on a track of vehicular width, you soon pass another remarkable waterfall where the torrent bursts out of a hole in the middle of a rock face.

When you arrive at the Hotel Waldhus (refreshments), go to the left of the building and on until confronted by the Schwarzbach, a stream almost as big as the Kander. Turn right along the river bank and at the confluence of the two rivers go left over a footbridge. Walking along the left bank of the Kander, and with rock walls to either hand, you are now in the Chluse Gorge. The river itself now gathers pace and erupts in some spectacular rapids.

Cross a bridge to the road on the other side and walk down it to the stone road bridge. Do not cross this one but keep down the right side of the raging river and cross the footbridge. Walk down the left side of Kander Falls (for that is what the river has become), and re-cross the river by yet another bridge.

You can now walk down to the lower station of the Gemmi cableway, where you can get a bus along to Kandersteg (SFr $1^1/_2$, no reduction to Half Fare Travel Card holders).

Walk 6 Kandersteg – Blausee – Mitholz – Büel – Kandersteg

Map nos:	Kandersteg Wanderkarte (1:25,000) Swiss Survey 263 (1:50,000), 1247 (1:25,000)
Walking time:	3 hours 45 minutes
Grading:	Easy walking from Kandersteg to Blausee with no exposure. The return is moderately strenuous with steep slopes to one side in places.
Highest altitude:	Saregrabe 1,310m (4,298ft)
Lowest altitude:	Blausee 887m (2,910ft)

The Blausee ('Blue Lake') is situated in the Kandertal about 3 miles below Kandersteg. It is a small lake, bright blue in colour, the intensity of which is chiefly due, it is claimed, to the exceptional purity of the water, which, incidentally, never rises above 10°Cin temperature, even in summer. The other outstanding feature is the number of trout it contains, some of which are quite huge. There is a trout breeding station close by, where the number of fish in various stages of development is quite extraordinary.

The walk from Kandersteg is down the valley bottom, never far from the river Kander. On the longer return leg the route meanders through Mitholz then climbs steeply to Hemlige after which it contours along the valley flank before descending towards Kandersteg. It should be explained that the railway up the Kandertal performs an 'S' bend in the neighbourhood of Mitholz in order to gain height. This is why the walking route crosses the railway three times within a short distance, the final time being over a tunnel.

The Walk

From Kandersteg railway station go in the 'down valley' direction (in other words, turn left on emerging) and after a few yards enter a surfaced path. Walk for a time with the river Kander to the right and the railway to the left, until eventually the path goes underneath the railway and main road. Beyond, at

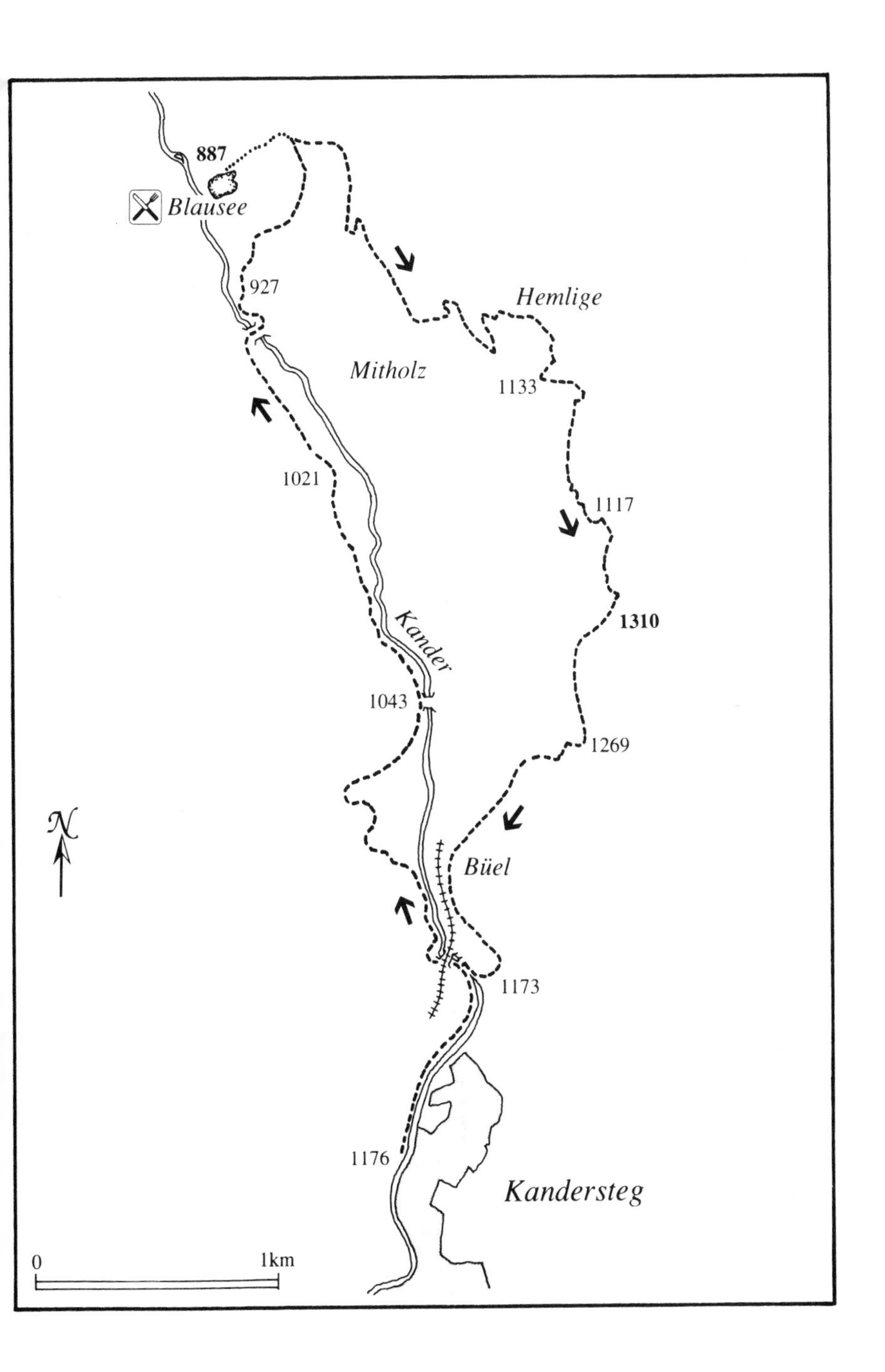
887
Blausee
927
Hemlige
Mitholz
1133
1021
1117
1310
Kander
1043
1269
Büel
1173
1176
Kandersteg
0
1km
N

the time of writing, there is a deviation left followed by two right turns back to the riverside (it is not clear whether this is a permanent or temporary detour). Follow the riverside now on a wider track. Veering slightly away from the river the track presently divides. Take the right branch and return to the river bank passing a bridge.

The river now veers away to the right and the track descends more steeply, with the town of Frutigen visible in the distance. At a T-junction turn right and soon cross the river. Follow the fairly level path until it emerges on to the main road. Turn left for 200m then left again to the entrance to Blausee. (Entrance fee SFr 3.50, which entitles you to wander at will, visit the trout breeding station and have a boat trip on the lake.) Walking round the lake with views of snowy summits including the Doldenhorn is very enjoyable and there are paths through rock-strewn woods. There is a fine restaurant within the complex where you can sample Blausee trout, among other things.

Returning to the main road, it is possible to catch a bus back to Kandersteg. To continue the walk, take the path opposite the Blausee car park and in a few metres turn right along a narrow road. After about 0.5km you can see the main road ahead, but 50m short of it you turn left under the railway, on a road that bends left then right to follow a course parallel to the main road. At a junction turn left and soon pass again under the railway (the middle part of an 'S' bend). Beyond the double bridge the road bends left towards Mitholz station. Just short of the station turn right and, in a few yards, right again. Walk along a level path to an attractive chalet. Here, where there is a level crossing over a siding to the right, bear left on a path that climbs steeply, bending to the left and then even further left so that you are now facing down the valley.

The path slants uphill in this direction and then zigzags up to Hemlige 1,120m (3,136ft). Bear right at a junction and soon the path levels with good views up valley. Keep right at the next junction of paths and you will soon round a corner to see the Stägebach ahead. This tumbles from above in a waterfall, and the stream then rushes between concrete piers which you have to step across.

At a fork take the left branch and climb steeply to a T-junction, where you go right. In a few metres cross a wooden bridge over a ravine, and shortly enter a 'V' gully and pass out the other side. Soon avalanche debris can be seen on the slopes above and a notice exhorts walkers to 'Keep moving'.

Cross a barrier and walk through woods to the next junction at Saregrabe. Bear right and go along a shelf below rocks and with steep slopes to the right. Pass through a gate, then follow the zigzags down through a wood as the path approaches the railway. Go through another gate and walk along a path

parallel to the railway tracks. When you come to th
the side until you see a path off to the right
cross the river and turn left on a path th
continue along the roadside into the
station.

During the latter part of the walk you w
to 'Nordrampe'. This is a walk devised by
goes from Ramslauenen, above the Kiental, to
here coincides with the Nordrampe route fro

Walk 7 Oeschinensee Chairlift – Unterbärgli and Oberbärgli – Hohtürli – Bundalp – Griesalp

Map nos:	Kandersteg Wanderkarte (1:25,000) (does not include Griesalp) Swiss Survey 264 (1:50,000), 1248 (1:25,000)
Walking time:	7 hours
Grading:	Strenuous. Exposed in places.
Highest altitude:	Hohtürli 2,778m (9,114ft)
Lowest altitude:	Griesalp 1,407m (4,616ft)

The Hohtürli has been a pass between the Kandertal and the Kiental for many years. It is the highest and arguably the most difficult of the 'walking' passes in the Oberland, and walkers with no Alpine experience are advised not to attempt this crossing in snowy or other adverse conditions.

The walk starts from the upper Oeschinensee chairlift station to which one rides from Kandersteg (SFr 6.60, 16 per cent reduction for Half Fare Travel Card holders). From here the route descends to and goes partly round the Oeschinensee, then climbs via Unterbärgli and Oberbärgli to the Hohtürli Pass, then down to Bundalp and on to Griesalp.

If you have to return to Kandersteg this can be achieved by getting a PTT bus from Griesalp to Reichenbach and then a train and BLS bus to Kandersteg. The bus ride from Griesalp to Reichenbach (SFr 14, 50 per cent reduction for Half Fare Travel Card holders) deserves a special mention. A series of tight hairpins has you marvelling at the skill of the driver as the bus descends from Griesalp to the valley bottom. There are walls of rock first to one side then to the other which the vehicle clears by inches, and glimpses of magnificent waterfalls as the Dündenbach tumbles down the mountainside. The bus trip takes 50 minutes and is good value.

Few trains that stop at Reichenbach will take you to Kandersteg, and you generally have to change at Frutigen. However, the BLS run a bus from the railway station at Frutigen to Kandersteg, included in the rail fare (SFr 8, 50 per cent reduction to Half Fare Travel Card holders).

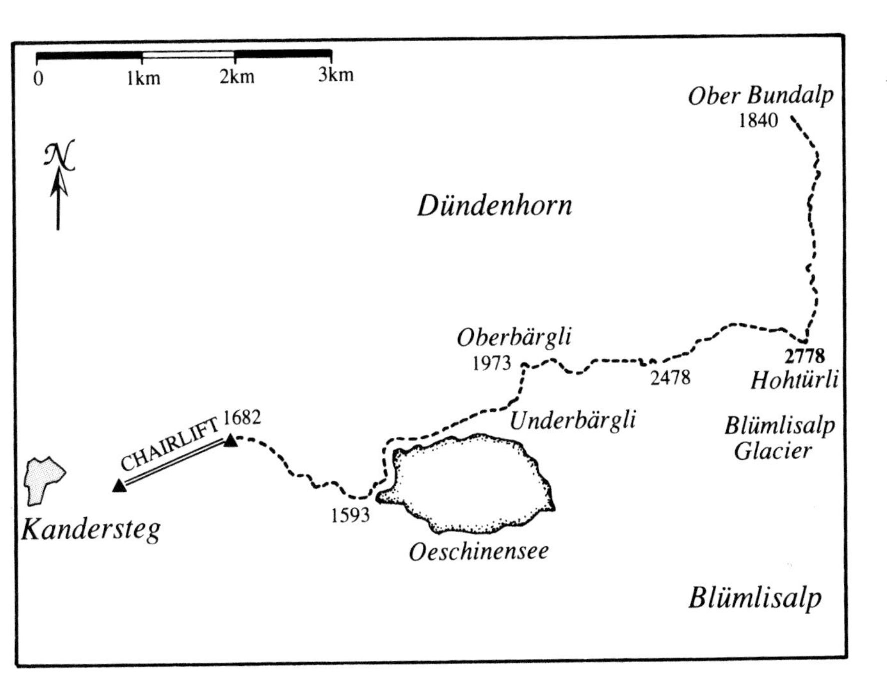

The Walk

From the chairlift station walk along the path signposted Oeschinensee and go straight across a four-way junction. (There is a path left at this point to the Hohtürli, but it is more scenic to go via the lake.) Walk down to the buildings near the end of the lake and follow the path that goes left round the shore. Bear left away from the lake at a signpost and start to climb. The path slants upward with overhanging rocks to the left, but no very steep gradients are encountered until you are above the chalets of Unterbärgli. Here a cliff is overcome by a stepped path that zigzags up with safety cables fixed in position. Above the cliff go through a rotary stile and approach the buildings of Oberbärgli (refreshments). This is a hive of farming activity. They have the usual cows, and also goats and pigs here.

Climb steadily on with masses of wild flowers to either side of the narrow path. Mountain masses are all around – the snowy peak that has dominated to the right is the Doldenhorn, with the Fründenhorn to the left of it. The peaks just to the right of 'in front' are part of the Blümlisalp. Looking behind, you will see the rugged Lohner group with the castle-like Tschingellochtighorn to the left.

Soon a steep uplift of scree-covered slopes is encountered. The path zig-

Heading towards the Hoturli Pass and the Blumlisalp Hutte

zags up it and, beyond, goes along the crest of an ancient moraine at a much more agreeable gradient. To the right, slopes fall precipitously to the Blümlisalp Glacier.

The moraine merges with the mountainside and the path continues at a fairly easy angle towards the final uplift, another steep scree slope. Twin tracks slant across it, with what seems to be an unofficial one-way system in operation. Take the left-hand furrow and plod up and across to the pass. There is not a lot of room here but the slopes to the right are broader and 150m up them is the Swiss Alpine Club's Blümlisalphutte (refreshments). This is a large stone building with 150 places to stay overnight, although many more than this have been accommodated in a crisis.

The Oeschinensee can be seen far below and the peaks of the Blümlisalp group dominate the view. Immediately above the mountain hut is the squat shape of the Wildi Frau and looking east the Bütlasse and the Gspaltenhorn are prominent.

Make no mistake: the route on the Kiental side is steep. Indeed, it is steeper for hundreds of feet than almost anything on the Kandersteg side. The path zigzags down a slope of unpleasant looseness with a wall of rock to the left. Safety cables have been fixed in places. Eventually the path comes down by a small glacier to the right and soon breaks away to the left. Cross a stream

On the Hotürli Pass, at 2,778m (9,114ft)

to gain the remains of an old moraine. The surface here is subject to erosion and the path is probably different from one year to the next. Where the moraine ends the path surface becomes more firm and soon a road is reached.

Turn left along the road but as you approach the restaurant at Bundalp (refreshments), take the path to the left of the building. Turn right, behind it, and through a gate then follow the path down to the road where you go left. Keep to the road until it bends sharply right. On the extremity of the bend go left on a level path for 0.5km. Where it 'tees' into another road, turn right and carry on down to a road junction where you bear left. Walk down round two hairpins then turn left down a *Bergweg*.

At a T-junction turn left and walk through trees. Cross a road and in a few metres you will emerge at Griesalp. On the side of the little village square are the Berghaus Griesalp and Chalet Hohtürli where refreshments are available. This is the starting point of the PTT bus service to Reichenbach, which leaves at 2.45, 4.45 and 6.45pm.

Walk 8 Kandersteg – Eggeschwand – Hotel Waldhus – Eggeschwand – Muggenseeli – Kandersteg

Map nos:	Kandersteg Wanderkarte (1:25,000) Swiss Survey 263 (1:50,000), 1247 & 1267 (1:25,000)
Walking time:	2 hours 15 minutes
Grading:	Easy. No exposure anywhere.
Highest altitude:	Hotel Waldhus 1,358m (4,455ft)
Lowest altitude:	Kandersteg 1,173m (3,848ft)

To the south of Kandersteg the river Kander reaches the end of the Gasteretal and cascades down the Chluse Gorge in spectacular fashion into the Kandertal. The walk comes to this point by way of the river bank, then goes up the narrow Gasteretal road to the upper Chluse Gorge. The route then crosses the rivers Kander and Schwarzbach to reach the Hotel Waldhus. Taking a different line back to the gorge, the walk goes down by the cascading river to Eggeschwand then returns to Kandersteg along the road.

The Walk

At Kandersteg railway station turn right to face up valley and walk along a road with the railway to your right. After a little more than 0.5km the road bends right, under the railway. Go straight over a four-way junction and walk with a graceful waterfall in view ahead. Keep left at the next junction, then, where the road to the Allmendalp cableway bears right, keep left on a fairly wide path that hugs the river bank. Eventually you will come to a complex of buildings that belong to the Scout movement. Past the last building turn right into meadowland. After passing through three gates, go left by a barn and, crossing the Alpbach, emerge on to a road. Go right and shortly turn sharply left on to a narrow road marked 'Gasteretal (Selden)'. This is not a public road but motorists may use it on payment of a toll; consequently, although there is no heavy traffic, you may see the odd car or two. The road climbs steeply with bare rock to the right and a substantial stone wall to the

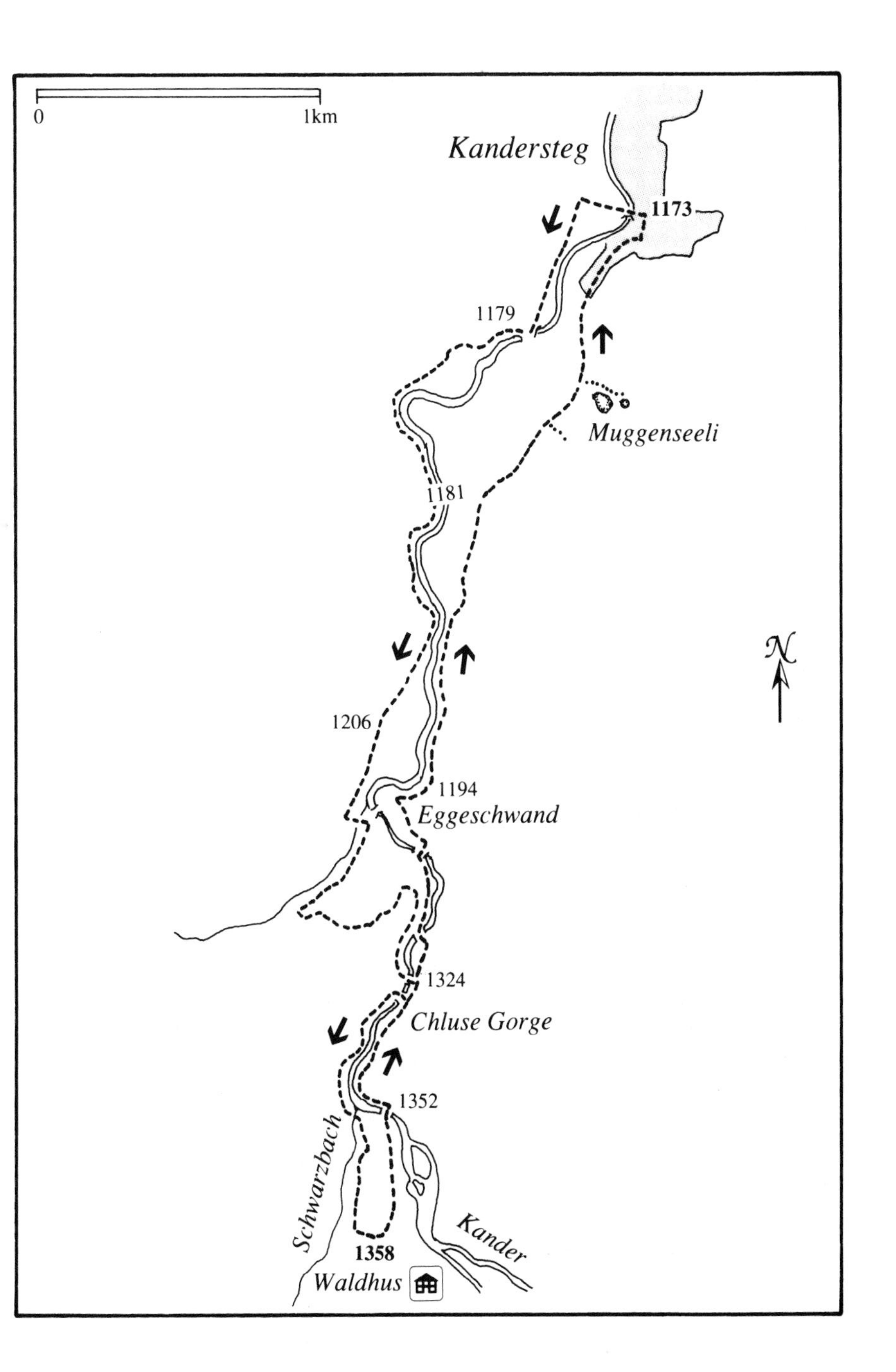
0
1km
Kandersteg
1173
1179
Muggenseeli
1181
1206
1194
Eggeschwand
1324
Chluse Gorge
1352
Schwarzbach
Kander
1358
Waldhus
N

Kandersteg

The River Kander in the Chluse Gorge

left. There are two short tunnels, so walkers should take care and hurry through.

Once you are through the second tunnel the river Kander can be seen foaming under the stone bridge ahead. You are now in the gorge of Chluse and the rock scenery is impressive. Across the river the cliffs rise almost vertically and on the near side rock overhangs the road. Cross the bridge, walk up the road and turn right across the next bridge. Go left and walk along the river bank past wild-looking rapids. Soon you will reach the confluence of the Schwarzbach with the Kander. Cross the smaller river by a footbridge and turn right to walk upstream.

Presently the path bends left to the Hotel Waldhus (refreshments). From here, you can look up the lower Gasteretal; you will not fail to be impressed by the mountain grandeur. The waterfall-streaked flanks are precipitous and very high.

Turn left along the road in front of the building and walk to the river Kander. Cross the bridge and turn left again. Follow the road back to the stone bridge but, instead of crossing it, go straight ahead on a path. Descend with the river thundering down the gorge to your left hand. A little way down, the path crosses the torrent by means of a wooden footbridge – it is a peculiar sensation to stand on the bridge and look upriver facing the cataract. Walking down the other side the impression of power becomes even greater as the gorge steepens and the Kander becomes a veritable waterfall.

Beyond the steepest part, turn right and cross another bridge, then follow the path down to the station of the Stock Gemmi cableway. You can, if you wish, get a bus from here to Kandersteg station (SFr $1^1/_2$, no reduction for Half Fare Travel Card holders).

If you walk along the road you will, in less than 0.8km, come to a bridge under the railway. There is a path to the left that goes past the Scout headquarters, so you can, if you prefer, retrace your earlier steps back along the river bank. If you walk on along the road for a little over 0.8km, just after passing the Hotel National, a small turning to the right will take you down to a quaint old watermill. This is a picturesque scene, with the stream running down to the wheel and the rock pinnacle of the Gallihorn forming a background.

Little more than 100m further on there is another turning immediately before the Hotel des Alpes. This gives access to the Muggenseeli, a delightful tarn with a small duck population and seats around. If you are lucky you may see the Gallihorn mirrored on its tranquil surface.

Resuming your route along the road, in 0.8km turn left to the railway station.

Walk 9 Sunnbüel – Gemmi Pass – Leukerbad – Gemmi Pass – Sunnbüel

Map nos:	Kandersteg Wanderkarte (1:25,000) Swiss Survey 263 (1:50,000), 1267 (1:25,000)
Walking time:	6 hours
Grading:	Easy. No real exposure. The descent from the Gemmi Pass is on a wide path, protected on the outside by cables on the exposed sections.
Highest altitude:	Gemmi Pass (cableway station) 2,346 m (7,697ft)
Lowest altitude:	Leukerbad 1,424m (4,672 ft)

The Gemmi Pass, linking Kandersteg with Leukerbad, has been used for centuries as a way over the main chain of the Oberland, being mentioned as early as 1252. Early tourists were carried up or down the 600m (2,000-ft) rock wall on the south side in sedan chairs, some with their eyes bound! The ascent or descent of this fantastic path is still quite sensational but improvements and the provision of safety barriers have made it safe for almost anyone. However, it is an advantage to have a steady head.

Since otherwise it would be quite a long day, we suggest the use of public transport at the start and finish of the walk – bus from Kandersteg to Eggeschwand and return (SFr 3, no reduction for Half Fare Travel Card holders), cable car from Eggeschwand to Stock and return (SFr 14, 20 per cent reduction for Half Fare Travel Card holders), chairlift from Stock to Sunnbüel and return (SFr 7, 20 per cent reduction to half price ticket holders). The latter offers only a dubious advantage and is included to avoid an end-of-afternoon scrabble to catch the last cable car down (5.30pm in summer). If you start early enough you could perhaps do without it; the first bus from Kandersteg station is at 8.30am. The walk from Stock to Sunnbüel is along a straightforward path and takes about 20 minutes each way.

Although strictly speaking only part of this route is in the canton of Berne (the remainder is in the Valais), the Gemmi is such an important geographical point as to merit inclusion in this collection. The proposed route goes across

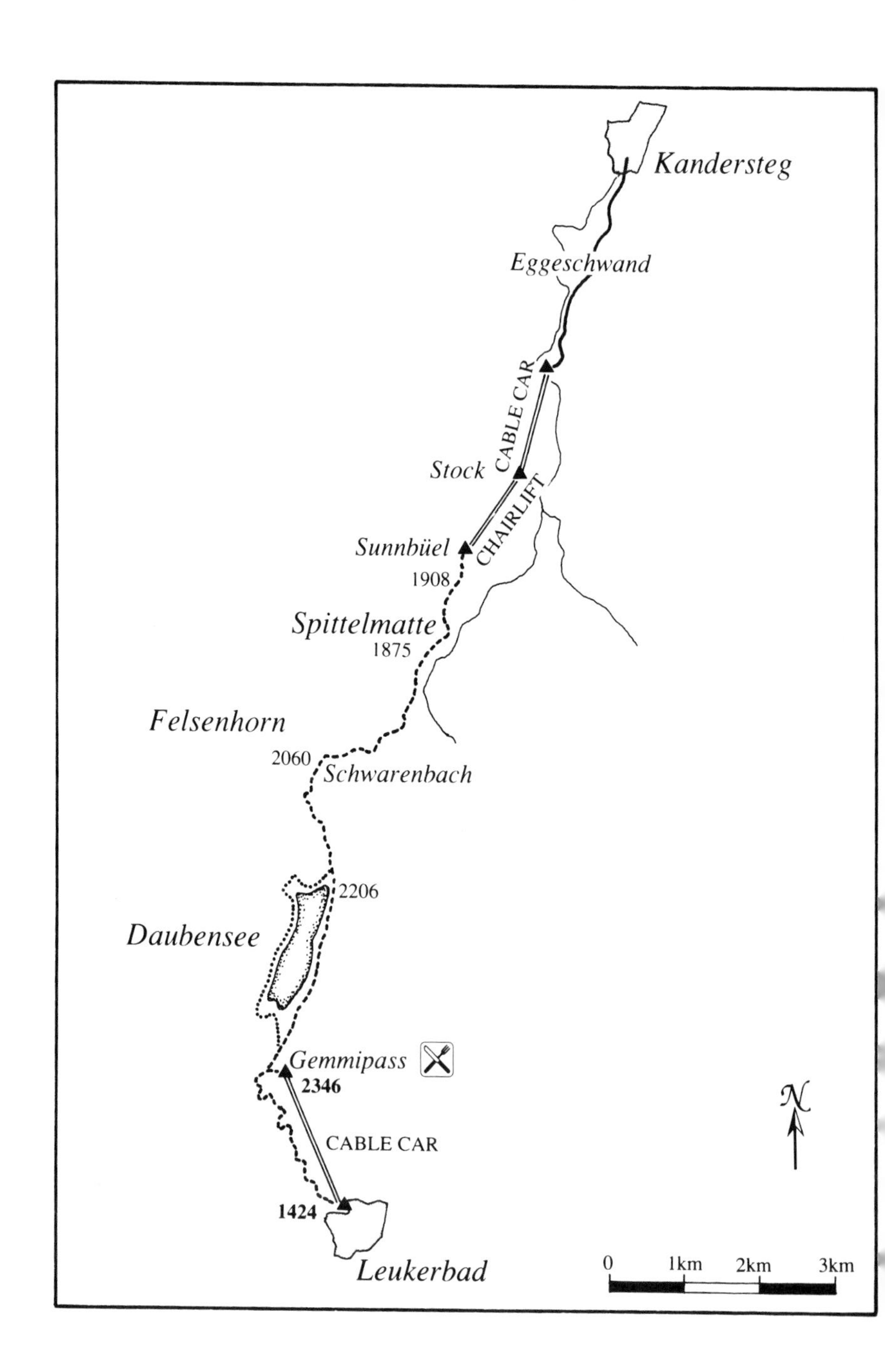
Kandersteg
Eggeschwand
CABLE CAR
Stock
CHAIRLIFT
Sunnbüel
1908
Spittelmatte
1875
Felsenhorn
2060
Schwarenbach
2206
Daubensee
Gemmipass
2346
CABLE CAR
1424
Leukerbad
N
0
1km
2km
3km

the broad plateau of Spittelmatte and on to the Gemmi Pass before descending to Leukerbad. It then ascends back to the Gemmi by cable car for the return to Sunnbüel along the same path (though this can be varied).

The Walk

Emerging from the chairlift station at Sunnbüel, turn left on the wide path signposted 'Gemmi'. Downhill at first, it levels out to cross the wide expanse of the Spittelmatte with the rocky ridge of the Ueschinengrat to the right and the bulk of the Altels on the left. Where a farm can be seen to the right of the track a path can be followed to the Arvenseeli, a delightful tarn surrounded by fir trees. This is only a few minutes' walk from the Gemmi track and, if you have the time, it is well worth the detour.

Only a short distance on from the junction is a plaque to the memory of six herdsmen. They and their herd of cattle were killed when part of the Altels Glacier broke away and avalanched in 1895.

The track now climbs with the Kleine Rinderhorn to the left. In fact, there is a choice of two tracks; it matters little which one you take. The *Alpenrose* grows in some profusion in this area, and there are many harebells and rock roses. After the track levels out you will soon reach the Schwarenbach, a mountain inn popular with walkers and climbers. The path swings left and climbs again to another level where the lonely Daubensee can be seen ahead. The Rinderhorn is now the mountain to the left while the peak at the far end of the lake is the Daubenhorn. Walk along the eastern (left) shore of the Daubensee on the path; half-way along, this starts to rise on the final uplift to the Gemmi.

The Hotel Wildstrubel on the pass provides accommodation and has a restaurant open to everyone. You will most likely prefer to diverge left to the viewpoint next to the cable car station – the panorama from the Gemmi is one of the most celebrated in the Alps. Leukerbad appears at an incredible depth below, and if you raise your eyes to the skyline you can, in clear skies, pick out the giants of the Mischabel, Monte Rosa, the Weisshorn, the Zinal Rothorn, the Matterhorn and Dent Blanche.

When you return to the path and begin to descend the great wall of rock towards Leukerbad, you will quickly appreciate what a well-engineered path it now is. Much concrete has been used in the construction of hundreds of steps, and twin lines of cable fixed to rigid metal posts protect the outside of the path wherever it is exposed to steep or vertical drops. The path zigzags down the cliff, sometimes with one section overhanging another below. There is little chance that you will find yourself alone on the cliff. On a

Descending towards the Daubensee

reasonably fine day there will be dozens of people of all ages walking up and down this unique pass.

Unfortunately, there will be little time to see Leukerbad. With the threat of that last cable car from Stock in mind, and the thought of a stop at the Schwarenbach on the return journey, you will probably want to return quickly to the Gemmi. The cable car station is only a little to the left of the path, and the service is quite frequent (SFr 12, with 50 per cent reduction to Half Fare Travel Card holders).

The return route is back along the same path. However, you can vary it by bearing left from the path and walking along the western side of the Daubensee. Hug the shore and regain the main track at the north-eastern corner of the lake. This diversion should not add more than 15 or 20 minutes to the walking time.

Walk 10 Kandersteg – Doldenhornhutte – Jegertosse – Kandersteg

Map nos:	Kandersteg Wanderkarte (1:25,000) Swiss survey 263 (1:50,000),1247 (1:25,000)
Walking time:	6 hours 45 minutes
Grading:	Kandersteg to Doldenhornhutte – moderate with negligible exposure. The remainder – strenuous and exposed in places.
Highest altitude:	Jegertosse 2,155m (7,070ft)
Lowest altitude:	Kandersteg 1,175m (3,855ft)

The Doldenhornhutte can be seen from Kandersteg, perched on its shelf, high up on the Doldenhorn massif. At first sight, it seems incredible that there could be a reasonably easy path up to it. The hut is the property of the Swiss Alpine Club and from it mountaineers climb the Doldenhorn to the south-east and the Fisistock to the south.

The Jegertosse is at the top of a rock buttress to the west of the Fisistock summits and directly above the lower Gasteretal. It is out of sight of Kandersteg itself.

This walk presents an opportunity of visiting a small mountain hut and perhaps taking a meal or other refreshment there. The route then goes across a precipitous face before climbing to Fisi Alp and on to Fisischafberg. From here it is a comparatively short distance to the fine viewpoint of Jegertosse. Returning to Fisischafberg, the route descends more or less directly towards Kandersteg.

The Walk

From Kandersteg railway station, go up to the main street and turn left as far as the bank where a wooden sign points to a side road opposite. Walk up this, mostly through trees, for about 1.5km then go right on a narrower path. Soon further progress seems to be limited by a cliff, but a gully presents a breach in the defences and the path zigzags up, with a fixed cable if needed. The path

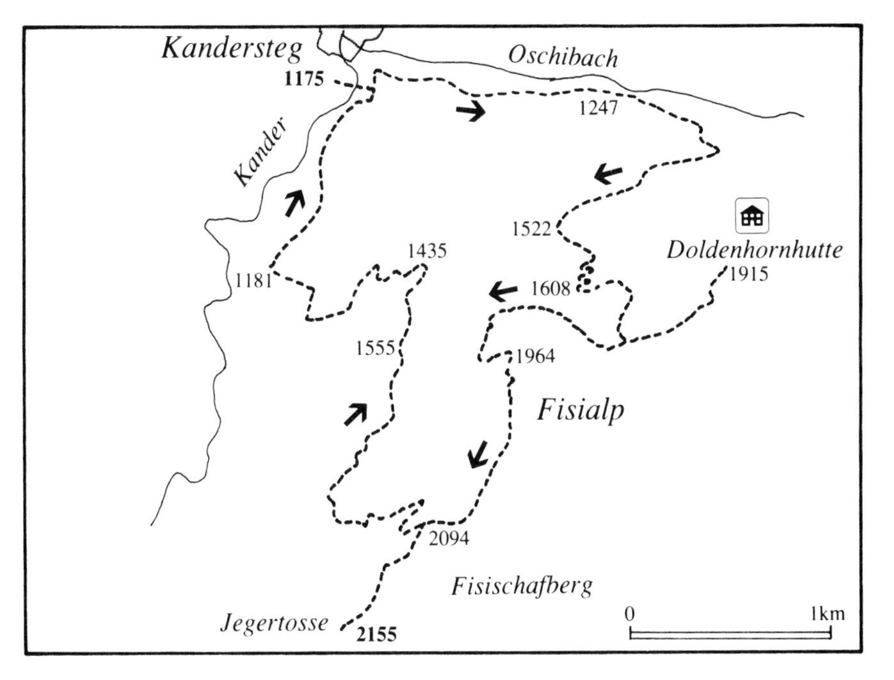

bears right and climbs steadily across the hillside, still through woodland, crossing a watercourse by means of a wooden bridge.

Cross another stream by a plank bridge and in a few yards turn left at a junction. This path becomes steeper and zigzags up, re-crossing the last stream. With the gradient easing, you will arrive at a T-junction where you turn left.

Soon the mountain hut can be seen ahead and in a comparatively short time you will walk up to it at 1,915m (6,283ft). Food and drink is obtainable here for quite reasonable charges – a cup of coffee is not only slightly cheaper but also larger than those to be had locally. It is very pleasant sitting on the terrace, sipping a drink and enjoying the view. Curiously, this is not the best place from which to see the Doldenhorn, which appears foreshortened, although a snowy peak is visible. The view into the valley however is impressive, with Kandersteg appearing far below.

From the hut, return to the T-junction and keep left. It can be seen from here that the route ahead is quite spectacular as walking routes go. As a matter of fact, the next part of the route looks more difficult than it actually is, but it is exposed for a short distance and a steady head is essential. The path approaches a rock wall of awe-inspiring height and climbs, following the base of the cliff. There are appreciable drops to the right but safety cables are in place and the path is wider than it looked from the junction. Once past the precipice on the right, the path begins to descend a kind of shelf, still with the rock wall to the left.

Eventually the path is joined by another coming from below; now the route begins to ascend again, and does so quite steeply for a time. Emerging into open Alp, the path comes up to the buildings of Fisi Alp at 1,973m (6,473ft). Farming is carried on here, although how they get animals in and out is a mystery.

The path slants leftwards across a grassy slope and is not too easily seen in places. Levelling out, the route passes through a rocky area and round the rim of a huge gully down which you may look towards Kandersteg. A lonely hut marks the junction of tracks at Fisischafberg.

Keep left and climb a stepped path to an area where construction work is being carried out. There are many avalanche barriers here and a private cableway connects it to the valley. Beyond, the path emerges on to fairly level ground and follows the edge of some sizeable cliffs before terminating on the Jegertosse, which itself has cliffs on three sides. This is a superb viewpoint. The Balmhorn and the Altels stand just across the Gasteretal with the Rinderhorn to the right of them. To the right of the Kleine Rinderhorn you can look along the length of the Schwarzbach valley towards the Gemmi Pass.

Return to Fisischafberg and, turning sharply left, begin to descend on a path that is at first of easy gradient. Soon that changes as the ground plunges towards the valley bottom. The path zigzags and is extensively stepped; in places it becomes a continuous stone staircase. The labour entailed in building it must have been immense. If you are lucky you may spot the lovely blooms of the Alpine columbine. This is a protected plant in Switzerland, and comparatively rare.

Eventually the path goes to the right and the gradient eases. Wooded areas alternate with clearings and in one of the latter a lonely chalet stands. Entering trees just beyond you come to the junction of Schleifen at 1,535m (5,036ft). Keep left here, and after a further descent through the forest turn left at another junction.

When you emerge from the trees for the last time, cross the valley bottom to the road and turn right. Walk along the road for a little more than 0.8km, then turn left to the railway station.

Walk 11 Kandersteg – Bütschels – Höh – Kandersteg

Map nos:	Kandersteg Wanderkarte (1:25,000) Swiss Survey 263 (1:50,000), 1247 (1:25,000)
Walking time:	2 hours
Grading:	Easy. Negligible exposure, except perhaps during the descent of the moraine.
Highest altitude:	Höh 1,335m (4,380ft)
Lowest altitude:	Kandersteg 1,175m (3,855ft)

About 150m (500ft) above Kandersteg the west flank of the Kandertal levels out to form a natural terrace. Below it, the ground falls abruptly, with much evidence of ancient glacial activity. It follows that along the edge of the terrace are a number of good viewpoints. There is a network of paths among the woods on the shelf and this walk contrives to take in the best of them and include part of the edge. The route goes south from Kandersteg to Bütschels from where it climbs through woodland to Höh. Coming to the edge and visiting a viewpoint, it then descends steeply to Kandersteg.

The Walk

From the railway station at Kandersteg turn right and go through the underpass to emerge on the other side of the railway. There is a broad flat space here, part of which is a road. On the far side is a wide path between fences. Go left along this with the railway to your left to a junction quite near the river Kander. Keep right and walk, with the graceful Waldrand waterfall straight ahead, through an area known as Bütschels. At the next four-way junction, go straight over on a green track. Opposite the Waldrand ski lift a road comes in from the left and with it a smoother surface. Soon a path goes left towards the waterfall, but keep right and climb through a conifer wood.

Emerging into open ground, bear left at a T-junction. At a four-way junction go straight over and into more forestry. At a T-junction go left and in a few metres arrive at another junction. Go straight over on to a very narrow *Bergweg*, which twists and turns through the forest, emerging by a

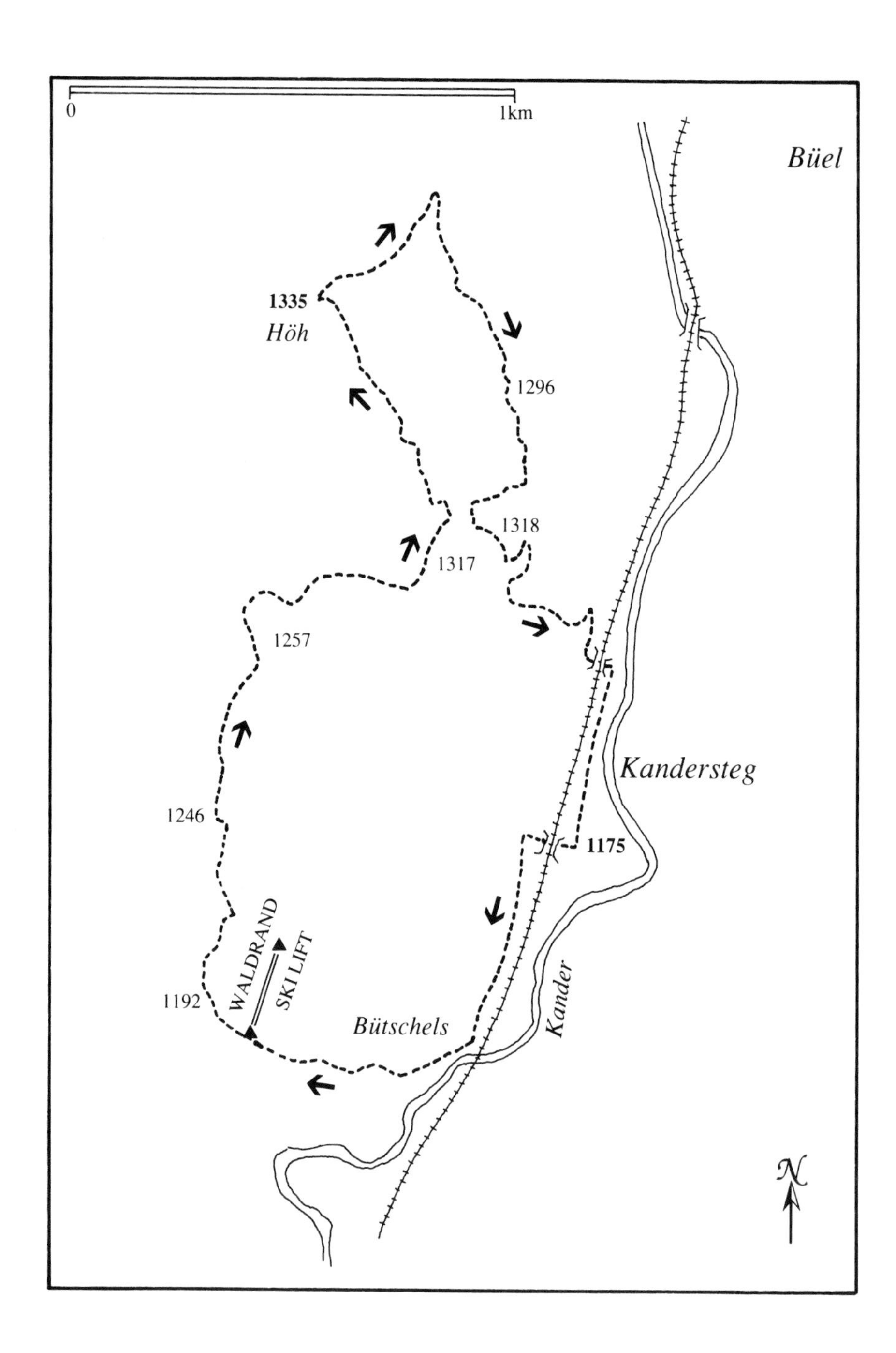
0
1km
Büel
1335
Höh
1296
1318
1317
1257
Kandersteg
1246
1175
WALDRAND
SKI LIFT
Kander
1192
Bütschels
N

The mist-shrouded peak of Bire above Kandersteg

barn. Go straight on at the junction just beyond to a four-way junction by a fence. Go through a gate in the fence and turn right, descending fairly steeply. At the junction at the bottom turn sharply right and begin to climb. Ignore a turning to the right and go on to the next junction where you become aware of the edge of the escarpment to the left. There are fine panoramic views to be had from here and the path keeps near the edge as you proceed in the same line. Ignore another branch to the right; soon the path draws away from the escarpment. At a T-junction go left and climb a bank to return to the edge.

This is probably the best viewpoint along the escarpment, with Kandersteg spread out below like a map. Beyond, you can look up the Oeschibach valley to the mountains at its head – the Rothorn, the Blümlisalphorn and Oeschinenhorn. Across the valley to the left, Bire is an impressive rock pyramid, while to the right the ridge from the Doldenhorn sweeps down to the peaks of the Fisistock and down to the Jegertosse.

The way down to Kandersteg is right in front of you. It starts along the crest of a rib, which is actually an ancient glacier moraine. The path keeps to the crest at first then zigzags steeply down the side. Near the bottom, go left at a T-junction with a broader track. Go down to the road and bear right, then shortly go left under the railway. Immediately beyond the underpass turn right on a path that will take you back to the railway station in a few minutes.

Walk 12 Niederhorn – Gemmenalphorn – Bareney – Habkern

Map nos:	Wanderkarte Berner Oberland Ost (1:50,000) Swiss Survey 254 (1:50,000), 1208 (1:25,000)
Walking time:	4 hours 15 minutes
Grading:	Moderate. Exposure not quite negligible. There are drops to the left of the Guggisgrat. Care should be taken just beyond the summit of the Gemmenalphorn.
Highest altitude:	Gemmenalphorn 2,067m (6,781ft)
Lowest altitude:	Habkern 1,055m (3,461ft)

To the north of Lake Thun rises the Niederhorn with the village of Beatenberg strung out along its southern flank. From the summit a fairly level ridge extends to the north-east over the Gemmenalphorn. The south-eastern slopes fall, comparatively gently, to the valley of the Lombach, where lies the developing resort of Habkern.

The walk starts from the upper station of the Niederhorn chairlift and goes along the crest of the long ridge. Beyond the Gemmenalphorn the route descends through pastureland and woodland to Habkern.

From Interlaken West you can travel to Beatenberg by PTT bus then ascend the Niederhorn by chairlift. As an alternative to the PTT bus and to lend variety to the journey you may consider taking a lake steamer from Interlaken West to Beatenbucht (there is one at 9.31am), then ascending the funicular to Beatenberg. From the top station there is a 20-minute walk to the chairlift that takes you to the top of the Niederhorn. This route takes about an hour longer than if you travel by PTT bus.

Travel back to Interlaken from Habkern also by PTT bus. (The single fares are Interlaken–Beatenberg SFr 6.20, chairlift SFr 12 and Habkern–Interlaken SFr 4.40. All prices are subject to 50 per cent discount to Half Fare Travel Card holders.)

The chairlift has been there since 1946 and there is an adjacent mountain inn with two restaurants.

Having arrived at the top station you will probably want to walk up to the summit (1,950m, 6,398ft) to enjoy the view. The most prominent feature is Lake Thun, far below, with the pyramid of the Niesen beyond it. The skyline is composed of all the major peaks of the Oberland – Wetterhorn, Schreckhorn, Finsteraarhorn, Eiger, Mönch, Jungfrau, Ebnefluh, Breithorn and Gspaltenhorn. Further to the right is the Blümlisalp, then the Doldenhorn, Balmhorn and Rinderhorn, and the Wildstrubel and Wildhorn can also be seen. On really clear days, Mont Blanc can be picked out between these last two mountains.

While in the vicinity of the summit you may see ibex, the mountain goats with long sweeping horns. They will normally be found on the western, more precipitous side of the mountain. If you don't see any here you are quite likely to during the next hour or two. They are part of the herd that is kept to between 80 and 100 animals. Ibex were reintroduced in 1949 after becoming extinct in this area.

The Walk

From the chairlift station take the path signposted 'Gemmenalphorn'. This goes behind the station building and round the flank of the mountain top, but

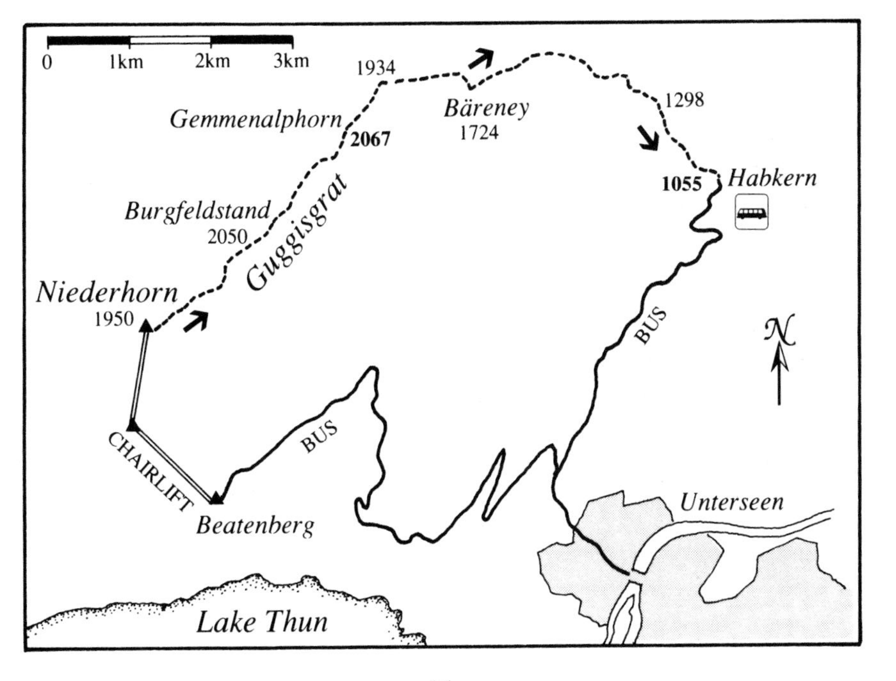

In the pastureland above Bareney

is soon on the broad crest of the ridge. The path is level and surfaced at first. After Hohsell, however, it is uphill to the summit of Burgfeldstand at 2,063m (6,768ft). The path is fairly wide and stepped where necessary, so you feel quite safe when admiring the tremendous precipices that fall away to the left. This is towards the valley of Justistal, on the other side of which is the serrated ridge of Sigriswilgrat.

The ridge you are on is known, collectively, as the Guggisgrat. Beyond Burgfeldstand, this narrows and undulates before reaching its highest point at the Gemmenalphorn. On either side of the peak, you may see ibex. They are not unduly perturbed by the presence of humans and will sometimes allow you to approach quite closely.

As the path leaves this summit, go down to the left before returning to the crest of the ridge. When the descending path reaches a col, turn right (but not sharply right) over ground inclined to be swampy. This is followed by a rocky area where the water-formed limestone has some crevasses, so tread carefully. The path now descends through pastureland where the going is again soft; reminiscent, indeed, of some British hill walking. Follow the path into a belt of trees and, on coming down to a small valley, go left and shortly keep left at a junction (signposted 'Chromatte and Habkern'). Go down through trees to a 'V' stile then walk through pastureland, carrying straight on past a barn. Go down a bank and cross a stream by a footbridge then descend another, steeper bank to 'tee' into a forest road.

Turn right and go through a gate then follow the road down, out of the trees and on to a junction at Allmend Lager. Habkern is now in sight below and beyond it the Harder ridge with the rock of Rotefluh prominent. Keep right, but a little way down leave the road and descend a grassy track to the left. Follow this down to a motor road where you turn right and walk down the road to the PTT bus terminus.

Walk 13 Wilderswil – Saxeten

Map nos:	Lauterbrunnental – Jungfrau Region Wanderkarte (1:33,333) Swiss Survey 254 (1:50,000), 1228 (1:25,000)
Walking time:	2 hours
Grading:	Fairly easy walking. No exposure anywhere.
Highest altitude:	Above Saxeten 1,120m (3,675ft)
Lowest altitude:	Wilderswil 584m (1,916ft)

The large village of Wilderswil lies at the foot of the Lütschine valley. In a south-westerly direction climbs the wooded valley of the Saxet, and where the valley floor becomes less steep is the village of Saxeten.

The walk is first on the south-east flank of the valley, then crosses the Saxetbach to the other flank where the path is narrow and steeper. The final approach to Saxeten is through open pastureland.

You can return to Wilderswil by the PTT service (usually in an adapted Land Rover), which runs at 1pm and 5pm during the summer months. It is possible to reserve seats by contacting the post office in Saxeten (tel: 22 20 21) and this is perhaps the safest thing to do (though not essential).

The Walk

Take the road by Hotel Christina, opposite Wilderswil's railway station and walk along for almost 0.8km to Barenplatz Square. There are some delightful chalets here, and some are quite old. Turn left at the square and go along to a road junction where the route goes right, signposted 'Saxeten'. (For Wilderswil Information Centre and change bureau you need to go beyond the junction for a few yards.) Having turned right, follow the road round to a T-junction where you turn right again and walk up to the Dorf Museum which is in the old mill building. The date 1513 can be seen on one of the beams and there is a restored waterwheel on the side.

The Saxetbach foams down past the mill over a boulder-strewn bed. Walk up the road on the southern bank, and where it bends in a hairpin to the left,

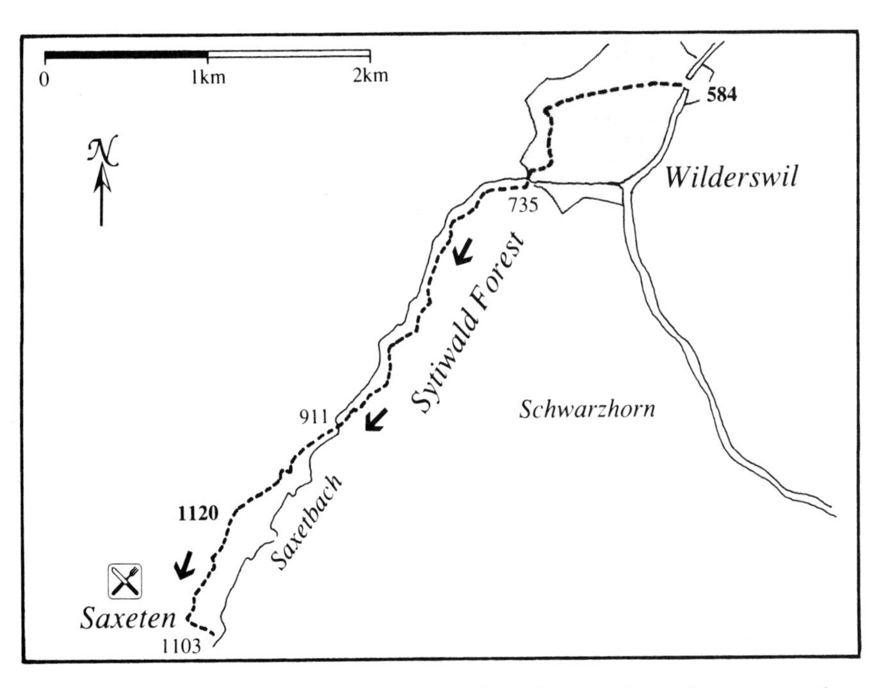

keep straight on, on a broad path. After a short distance the path narrows and at this point go left up some steps to regain the road. Walk up it to the next hairpin and follow the path that leaves the road to the right.

This fairly wide path climbs steadily through the Sytiwald Forest. Keep left at a fork and continue to climb through woodland that is mostly broad-leaved, with plenty of beech. Only occasionally you get a glimpse of the Saxetbach as the height of the path above the river increases. Eventually the path levels out, but so steep is the valley bottom that soon the height difference between river and path is almost wiped out. In places the path has slipped locally and two wooden bridges have been installed over gaps. At another landslip the path has been diverted around the gap.

Where the route crosses the Saxetbach the remains of the original bridge lie around in disarray. In recent history it must have been destroyed by storm and a two-piece wooden structure is now in position. A seat has been provided on the north-western bank; this is a welcome sight for some on an otherwise seatless route.

On the other side of the river the path is narrower and the character of the scenery changes. Dense forest gives way to areas of open Alp bright with wild flowers, and several small footbridges are encountered. There are bands of woodland through which the gradient increases, and here the path has been

A bridge on the path to Saxeten

engineered with zigzags and steps. Eventually the path crosses a final footbridge and ascends a last flight of steps to emerge on to open meadowland.

Cross a grassy area towards two barns where the route joins another track. Bear left and walk along this wider, level way towards the village of Saxeten with views of the Schwalmere at the valley head in front. If you are in need of refreshment the Hotel Alpenrose will be a welcome sight.

For the PTT terminus turn left for about 150m.

Walk 14 Wilderswil – Bonigen – Iseltwald – Giessbach

Map nos:	Wanderkarte Berner Oberland Ost (1:50,000) Swiss Survey 254 (1:50,000), 1208, 1209 & 1228 (1:25,000)
Walking time:	5 hours (including up to Giessbach Falls and down to jetty)
Grading:	Easy walking. No exposure anywhere.
Highest altitude:	Giessbach Falls 760m(2,493ft)
Lowest altitude:	Shore of Lake Brienz 564m (1,850ft)

Since the twin lakes of Thun and Brienz are such important features of the Bernese Oberland it seems appropriate that at least one lakeside walk should be included here. This one starts as a riverside walk, following the Lütschine from Wilderswil to Bonigen. The route then takes in almost the entire southern shore of Lake Brienz, finishing at the spectacular Giessbach Falls. Afterwards the walker may return down the lake by steamer.

The Walk

From Wilderswil railway station turn left and walk towards the tower of Gsteig church. Cross the old covered bridge and immediately turn left on to the Lütschinen Promenade. Climb slightly to go round a nursery then walk along the right bank of the river to a junction. Turn left to cross the river by another covered bridge and turn right to walk along the left bank. There is a footpath right on the brink, with a road running parallel a few yards to the left.

Turn right over a concrete road bridge and keep on in the same line through Bonigen. When you emerge by the lakeside, walk on along the south shore of Lake Brienz. This part of the route is a road walk, but it is along a quiet road that hugs the shore till it climbs to the village of Sengg before descending towards Iseltwald, a pleasant summer resort on a small peninsula. Turn left down a path, then bear right towards the pier. By the Hotel Bernahof bear

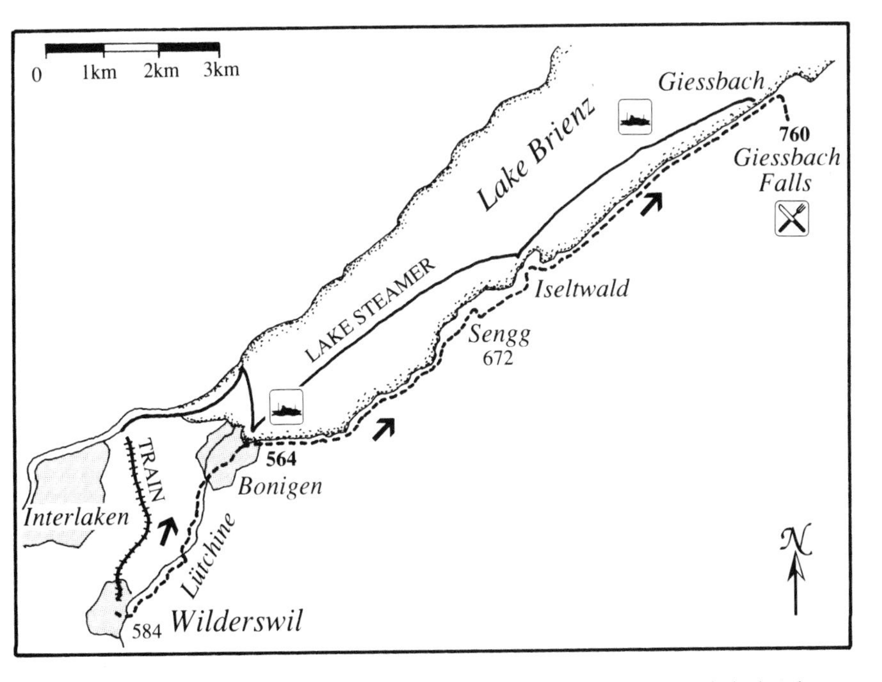

right again. Enter a narrow road that passes the front of residential chalets by the lakeside. At the end of the village bear left on a path that goes right to the water's edge.

This is lakeside walking at its very best. The path is right by the water's edge at first, with woodland covering the steep slopes to the right. A rocky headland is passed by means of a tunnel, then the path begins to undulate but is never far from the shore. At one point it passes under an overhang, then climbs between rocks to a picnic site with a shelter before descending through a beech wood back to the lakeside.

Eventually, ahead and at some height above the lake, you will see a striking building amongst the dense woodland. This is the Park Hotel Giessbach, long established in its position near Giessbach Falls. As the path advances you can turn right on a path signposted 'Giessbach Hotel', a climb of 15–20 minutes. If you keep to the lakeside path you will come to a left-hand branch that goes via a short tunnel to the jetty where the lake steamers call. Here, also, is the lower station of a funicular railway that rises to the hotel. (SFr 4.20 return or SFr 2.80 one way, no reduction for Half Fare Travel Card holders.) It is a quaint transport system, having been in existence since 1879, the second oldest funicular railway in Switzerland.

At the hotel there is a terrace where you can have meals or drinks, but the

The paddle steamer 'Lotschberg' on Lake Brienz

main attraction is the waterfall. This is really a gigantic series of cascades that begin 350m (1,150ft) above the lake. You can see the greater part of these from the hotel, but to get a closer look, walk up a path on the nearer side. Pause at the first bridge and enjoy the sight of the cataract as it plunges towards you, then go up to the next bridge which crosses the ravine behind one of the cascades.

There is an alternative path that zigzags down towards the lake then left to the jetty. This enables you to see the final cascade of Giessbach Falls as it discharges into the lake. Whether on foot or by tram, be there in time to catch a steamer back to Interlaken (last one at 6.22pm). Tickets may be purchased on board, and the voyage to Interlaken Ost takes about an hour.

Walk 15 Schynige Platte – Faulhorn – Bachsee – First

Map nos:	Wanderkarte Berner Oberland Ost (1:50,000) Swiss Survey 254 (1:50,000), 1228 & 1229 (1:25,000)
Walking time:	6 hours
Grading:	Strenuous. Exposure is minimal except where the track rises steeply just beyond the Weber hut. Care should be exercised on the summit of the Faulhorn which has precipices on its east and north sides.
Highest altitude:	Summit of Faulhorn 2,681m (8,796ft)
Lowest altitude:	South of Loucherhorn 1,904m (6,247ft)

Between Lake Brienz and the Lütschental, in which Grindelwald lies, rises a compact mountain mass. Not high by Alpine standards (none of the summits reach 3,000m) it is, nevertheless, a wild rocky area and snow can persist in places well into the summer. At its western end, Schynige Platte looms above Interlaken. A rack and pinion railway climbs from Wilderswil to the summit. It was opened in 1893 and, although it is now electrified, the journey still takes 52 minutes. Used mostly by visitors to the renowned Alpine Garden at Schynige Platte, which has more than 500 varieties of mountain flowers, the railway is a convenient way for walkers to gain access to this delightful region.

On the eastern side a long chairlift descends from First to Grindelwald, from where you can get a train back to Wilderswil or Interlaken.

It is possible to purchase an all-in ticket that includes ascent of the Schynige Platte railway, descent from First to Grindelwald and the return by train. From Wilderswil this costs SFr 38, subject to a 50 per cent discount to holders of the Half Fare Travel Card.

The walking route is a high-level one, never dropping below 1,900m (6,234ft) and heading generally eastwards. On the way it passes the diminutive Weber Hutte then goes on to the summit of the Faulhorn at about two-thirds distance. It then descends to a delightful tarn, the Bachsee, and on to First.

The Walk

At Schynige Platte station walk back down the platform, go left to cross the railway and left again, down a wide path. Shortly, bear left on to a narrower path and go straight over a junction, walking in the direction of the rocks of the Oberberghorn.

On reaching the rocks go right at a T-junction. You will now be on the *Panoramaweg* and will soon be walking near the edge of precipices falling away to the north-west. The way is protected, so there is no danger and stupendous views of Interlaken and Lakes Thun and Brienz are your reward. The small townships of Bonigen, Ringgenberg and Niederried can be seen as on a map and, looking down Lake Thun, Spiez is easily picked out. On the other side of Lake Brienz is the ridge that rises from Harderkulm, with the Augstmatthorn looking very different from the profile seen from lake level. Further away is the Niederhorn (with a pylon on its summit) and the long ridge from it to the Gemmenalphorn.

The *Panoramaweg* passes several viewpoints then gradually draws away from the edge as it climbs. At one point you have to descend a metal stairway, but shortly after this you join the main Faulhorn track which climbs steeply for a short distance then bends right, round the slopes of the Loucherhorn.

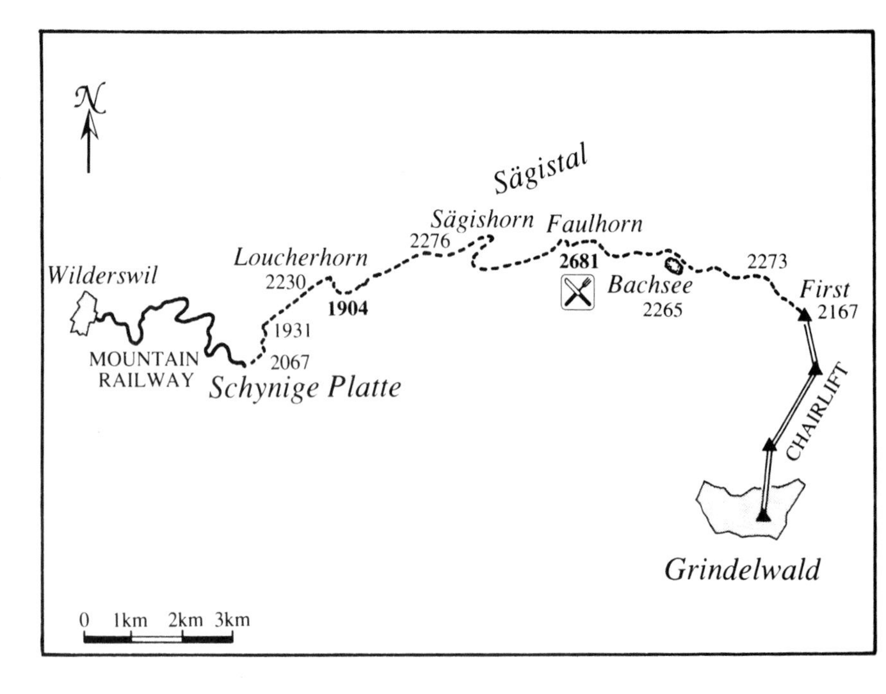

Beside Bachsee. To the right of the Schreckhorn is the Finsteraarhorn

The track descends now to its lowest point with a rock-strewn valley down to the right, then begins to climb with the rocky mass of the Sagishorn ahead. It bears to the left of this and reaching a saddle starts a long slant across the southern flank of the Sagistal, at a more gentle angle. There are sheep in this valley (not a common sight in the high Alps) and notices have been seen advising visitors to 'Beware of the Ram'! To the left, in the valley, is the turquoise Sagistalsee and at one point a glimpse of Lake Brienz beyond.

Rounding the ridge from the Sagishorn, the path bends sharply right and the Faulhorn suddenly appears with the Swiss flag flying near its summit. The way becomes more rocky and can be slippery when wet. You soon come up to the Weber Hutte (refreshments) at 2,344m (7,690ft). There is a branch to the right here that you may take if the weather has deteriorated or conditions turn out worse than expected. This eventually descends to Burglauenen where there is a station on the Grindelwald–Interlaken railway. Otherwise, bend left round the hut and climb steeply up slabby rocks where there are fixed cables.

Above this steep pitch the track turns to head directly towards the Faulhorn. It progresses in a series of steps; long, almost level sections interspersed with steeper uplifts. You eventually emerge on to a ridge which narrows as the final peak looms ahead. When you arrive under the summit there is a steepish zigzag path to climb, but the added incentive of the hotel (restaurant and refreshments) just below the top will spur you on.

There are glorious views in all directions from the summit. Most of the Oberland giants can be seen – Wetterhorn, Schreckhorn, Finsteraarhorn, Eiger, Mönch, Jungfrau, Grosshorn, Breithorn, Tschingelhorn, Gspaltenhorn and Blümlisalp. The Schilthorn is in view, and, further away, the flat-topped Wildstrubel. To the east, the lopsided Titlis is recognisable among a multitude of peaks. Nearer at hand, the Schwarzhorn group of summits is prominent.

Descend from the front of the hotel and walk down the track that goes down the valley to the left of the prominent peaks of Simelihorn and Reeti. Bear left at a junction and, a little later, ignore a branch to the left. Head for the Bachsee, the picturesque small lake lower down the valley, passing the Bergener shelter at 2,438m (7,999ft). The Bachsee, 2,265m (7,431ft) is a deservedly popular beauty spot where the waters of the lake and the cows that graze round it make a suitable foreground to the icy peaks beyond.

The track goes round the north shore and passes another shelter, intended for walkers caught by bad weather. It then continues in an undulating manner towards the top station of the First chairlift (refreshments).

Footnote It is possible that by the time you read this the Grindelwald–First chairlift (at the time of writing the longest in Europe) will have been converted to a Gondelbahn, with enclosed gondolas replacing the double chairs.

Walk 16 Mürren – Schilthornhutte – Schilthorn Summit

Map nos:	Lauterbrunnental – Jungfrau Region Wanderkarte (1:33,333) Swiss Survey 264 (1:50,000), 1248 (1:25,000)
Walking time:	4 hours 15 minutes up (3 hours down)
Grading:	Strenuous (going up), moderate (descending). Exposure is minimal (this does not apply if there is a significant amount of snow).
Highest altitude:	Schilthorn summit 2,971m (9,747ft)
Lowest altitude:	Mürren 1,634m (5,361ft)

Mürren is reached from Lauterbrunnen by taking the funicular to Grutschalp, then what is known as an adhesion railway along to the famous mountain resort.

The Schilthorn rises to the west of the village. It became famous after being chosen as the setting for the James Bond film *On Her Majesty's Secret Service*, and from this derived its other name 'Piz Gloria'.

The walk passes the Sonnenberg restaurant on its way to the Schilthornhutte. It then goes up the Engital then climbs to the summit of the Schilthorn by way of the south-east shoulder.

A funicular links Mürren with the summit of the Allmendhubel, a hill above the village, and this could be used as a start, saving 30–40 minutes of walking time.

The Walk

From Mürren railway station turn left and walk south along the main street. After less than ten minutes turn right past a bakery and walk up a narrow road. With some bends this negotiates the steep slopes to the Restaurant Sonnenberg. Passing this building to the left you can take a path that swings right to join another narrow road. Follow this up to a saddle, with the Allmendhubel to the right. At the junction on the saddle turn left on a wide track and soon go over an unusual stepped stile. The going now gets steeper as you climb with the Ägertenbach stream to the right. The slopes to the left are part of the peculiarly shaped Muttlernhorn.

As you top a brow you will see the Schilthornhutte ahead at 2,432m (7,979ft); this belongs to Mürren Ski Club but is kept open during the summer months. Roughly half-way up, it enjoys a strategic situation and many stop here for food and drink. Beyond is the Engital, a rather barren-looking valley, and the route goes up the right flank of this. On the col at the upper end keep right at a junction and walk up a wide track with the tarn of Grausee in the hollow to the left.

The peak of the Schilthorn is now in full view ahead, and the rocky ridge high on your right is the Schwarzgrat. Swinging left to cross the head-waters of the Schiltbach the route gets steeper as it passes under the cables of the Schilthorn cableway and heads for the south-east shoulder of the mountain. Just below the shoulder, bear right across the rocks to the ridge and follow it to the summit. Much of the space at the summit is taken up by the famous revolving restaurant. At the time of writing, much construction work is going on to improve the complex of buildings. The continuously revolving restaurant is being enlarged to increase the seating accommodation from 216 to 448 places. James Bond's heliport will be converted to a Touristorama combining an observation terrace with a building that has banquet and seminar facilities. Everything else is being refurbished. By the time you read this, all these modifications should be completed.

The view from the existing terrace is magnificent. Most of the Oberland giants can be seen, from the Wetterhorn through the Eiger, Mönch and Jungfrau to the Blümlisalp and Doldenhorn. The Gspaltenhorn seems quite near across the Sefinental, and Bütlasse is just to the right of it. In the opposite direction you can look down the length of the Saustal with the Schwarzgrat to the right, partitioning it from the Engital up which you so recently toiled. Right of that is Birg crowned by the intermediate station of the Schilthorn cableway. You will see this at closer quarters if you elect to descend by cable car.

The Luftseilbahn Stechelberg–Mürren–Schilthorn (LSMS), to give it its official name, was completed in 1967. It is the longest Swiss cableway, 6,931m (22,740ft) in length, and having a total ascent (from Stechelberg, in the valley below Mürren) of 2,103m (6,900ft). The one-way fare to Mürren is SFr 26 (subject to 50 per cent discount if you have a Half Fare Travel Card).

If you prefer to walk down, retrace the ascending route as far as the junction near the head of the Engital, where you go right. Keep to the left of Grausee, crossing the Schiltbach as it emerges from the lake.

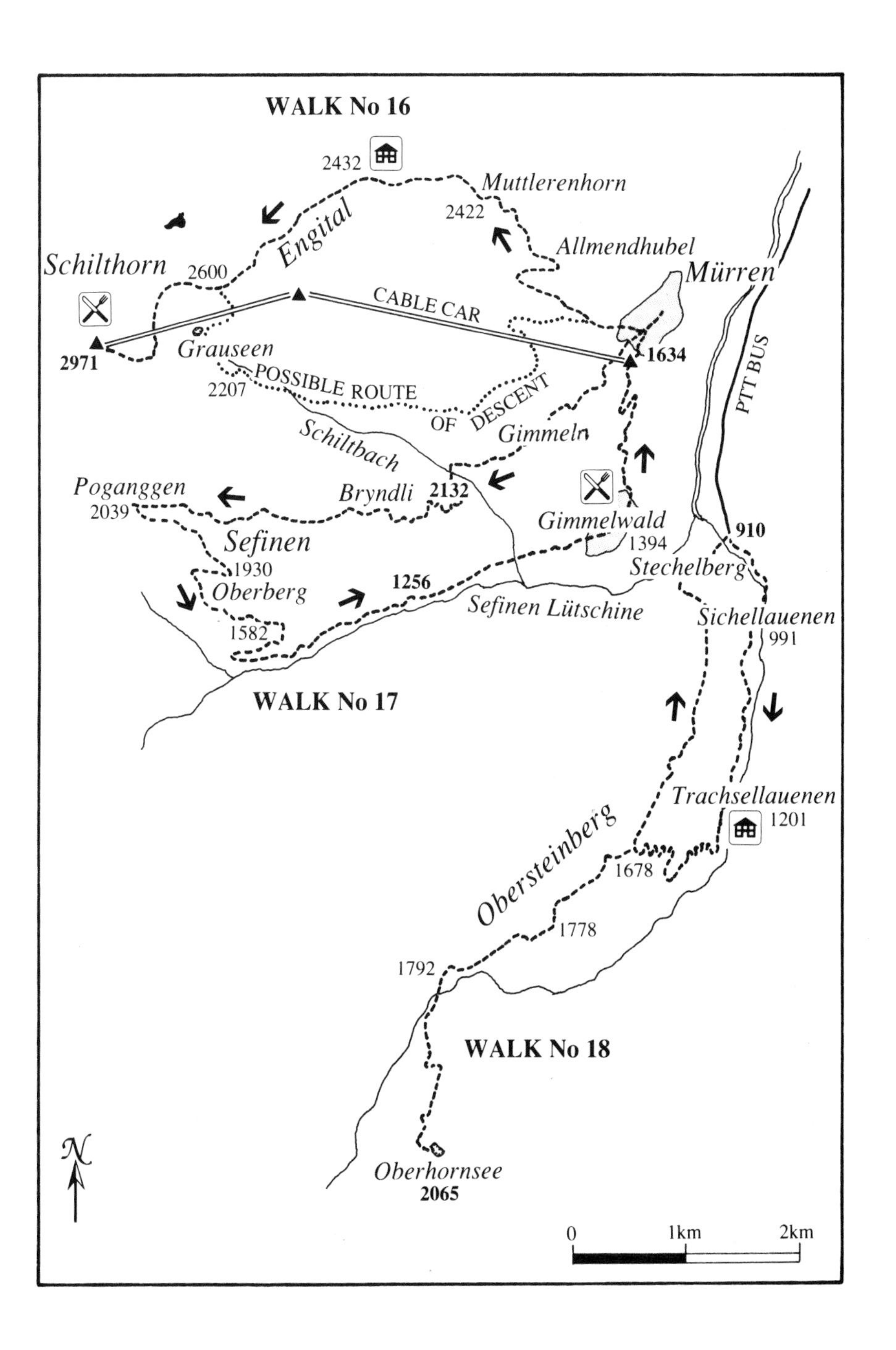
WALK No 16
2432
Muttlerenhorn
2422
Engital
Allmendhubel
Schilthorn
2600
Mürren
CABLE CAR
Grauseen
2971
1634
PTT BUS
POSSIBLE ROUTE
OF DESCENT
2207
Schiltbach
Gimmeln
Poganggen
2039
Bryndli
2132
Gimmelwald
910
Sefinen
1394
1930
Stechelberg
Oberberg
1256
Sefinen Lütschine
Sichellauenen
1582
991
WALK No 17
Trachsellauenen
1201
Obersteinberg
1678
1778
1792
WALK No 18
N
Oberhornsee
2065
0
1km
2km

The Eiger towering above Mürren

On the Mürren to Poganggen path with, to the right, the Eiger and Mönch

Go left at a junction and descend, re-crossing the Schiltbach then gradually edging away from the stream. Disregard branches to the right and contour round the mountainside to come down by the restaurant at Suppenalp. Go right here and descend towards Mürren, meeting the route of ascent above the village.

Walk 17 Mürren – Gimmeln – Spielbodenalp – Poganggenalp – Sefinental – Gimmelwald – Mürren

Map nos:	Lauterbrunnental – Jungfrau Region Wanderkarte (1:33,333) Swiss Survey 264 (1:50,000), 1248 (1:25,000)
Walking time:	5 hours 30 minutes
Grading:	Moderate. Not exposed anywhere.
Highest altitude:	Bryndli 2,132m (6,995ft)
Lowest altitude:	Im Tal 1,256m (4,121ft)

To reach Mürren from Lauterbrunnen, *see* Walk 16.

The first part of this walk is along the usual path to the Sefinenfurgge (the mountain pass to the Kiental). From Mürren it climbs to Gimmeln, crosses the Schiltbach brook then climbs again to Bryndli. A fairly level path to Poganggen is followed by a descent to the Sefinen Lütschine river. After a riverside walk comes a steady climb through Gimmelwald to Mürren. At Gimmelwald the walk may be shortened by taking the cable car to Mürren, or, if preferred, down to Stechelberg.

The Walk

From Mürren railway station, go left on emerging and walk along the main street passing the Schilthornbahn station. The road begins to climb, turning right where another track goes straight on and entering a band of trees. Above the trees the way becomes level at Gimmeln where the display of wild flowers is a delight to the eye in early summer. The number of different species has to be seen to be believed, and cornflowers, campions, globe flowers and pansies are just a few of the many.

Keep left at a junction and walk down towards a group of old huts, with the Schilthorn and Birg showing up ahead and to the right. Turn left through a gate and descend to a footbridge over the Schiltbach. A climb up the other side brings you to Spielboden Restaurant at 1,793m (5,883ft) where you bear left. Keeping the buildings to your right, ascend a narrow path. The buttress of Bryndli towers overhead and the path zigzags up it in what is the most strenuous part of the route. At the top stop and look at the tremendous view. Behind are Jungfrau, Mönch and Eiger with the latter presenting its most spectacular profile from this angle. To the left the great wall of the Oberland is topped by the peaks of Ebnefluh, Mittaghorn, Grosshorn and Breithorn.

The path is fairly level now. Keep right where it forks and contour across the mountainside. To the left the Gspaltenhorn, supported by the jagged Tschingelgrat, becomes the main feature. Ahead the Hundshorn, northern bastion of the Sefinenfurgge Pass begins to loom. The Schilthorn looks quite close on the right and a track towards it comes in at a junction. However, you continue in line and soon you will see the Rotstockhutte ahead. One of three buildings at Poganggen, the Rotstockhutte is owned and run by the Stechelberg Ski Club but members of the public may use it. (Meals and *Matratzenlager* accommodation are available.)

Here we leave the Sefinenfurgge path and turn sharply left before reaching the stream. Crossing the mountainside and fording several streams this new path loses height only gradually at first. The buildings of Oberberg, which you probably saw from the higher path, can be seen ahead. This is a dairy farm that is prosperous enough to have its own cableway. The pleasant sound of cowbells greets you as you come down to a junction of paths and turn right across open ground where orchids grow.

This is a good vantage point from which to study the great face below the crest of the Tschingelgrat across the valley. You are quite likely to see falls of ice and snow which are accompanied by a rumble rather like thunder. Remember though, that sound travels rather more slowly than light, so if you hear the rumble you may have missed the main fall. After a bend to the left the path becomes much steeper and rather unpleasantly loose. Where it bends right, past the huts of oxen you have to negotiate one of those three- (or four-) bar structures they use instead of gates in these parts. The bars are completely removable, so make sure they are back in place after you've passed. Another of these has to be negotiated lower down as you approach the valley bottom.

Sound-effects from the Sefinen Lütschine river that foams down this valley will already have reached your ears. A left-hand bend and further descent bring you to an exhilarating walk along its bank. At one point, even in late summer, you may see the torrent disappear under a snow bridge for some metres.

The sight of buildings ahead and the sound of cowbells tell you that you've arrived at Im Tal, a farm with a three-barred 'stile' on each side of it. Just

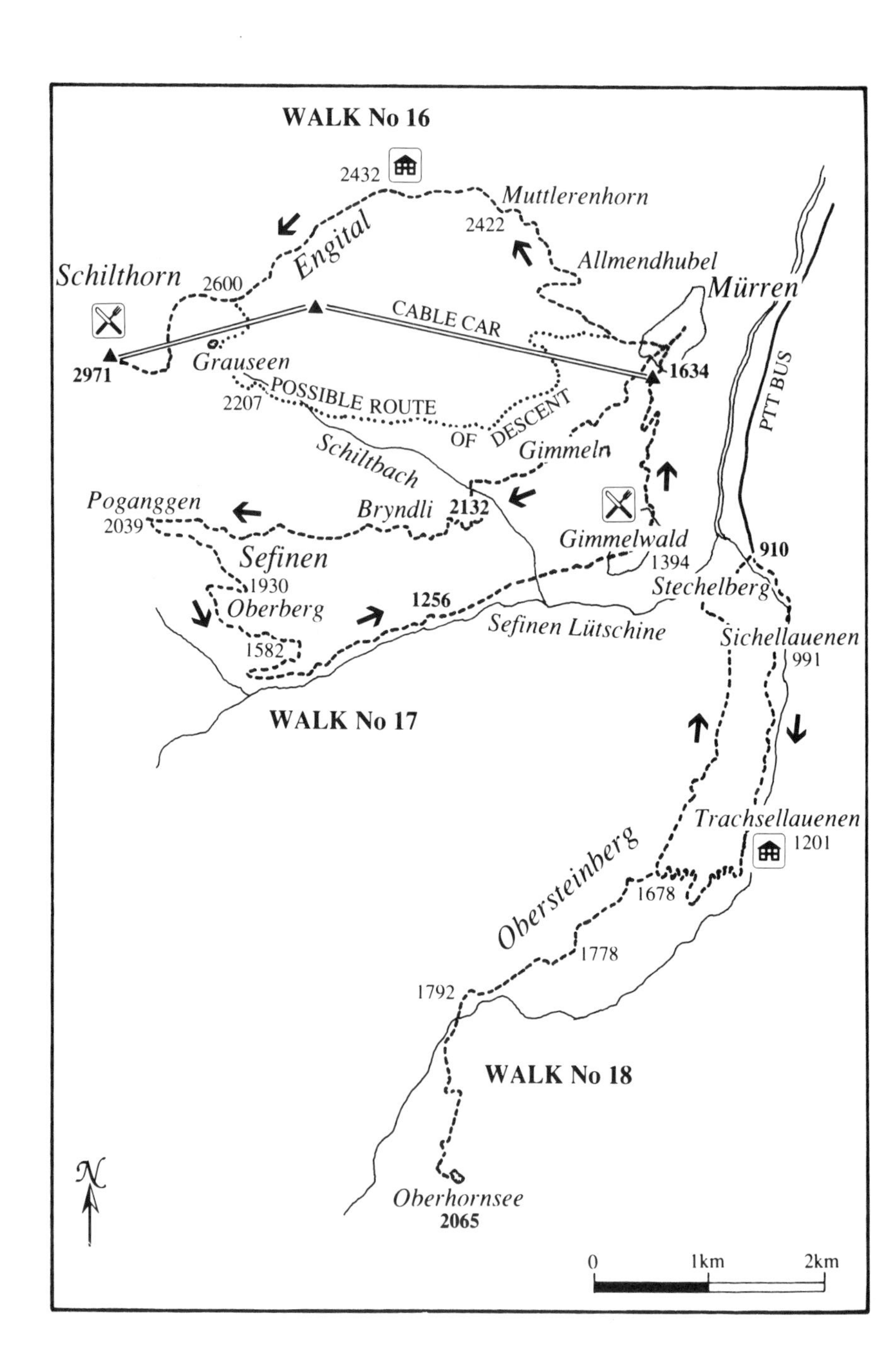

WALK No 16
2432
Muttlerenhorn
2422
Engital
Allmendhubel
Schilthorn
2600
Mürren
CABLE CAR
Grauseen
2971
1634
POSSIBLE ROUTE
2207
OF DESCENT
PTT BUS
Schiltbach
Gimmeln
Poganggen
2039
Bryndli
2132
Gimmelwald
Sefinen
910
1394
1930
Stechelberg
Oberberg
1256
Sefinen Lütschine
Sichellauenen
1582
991
WALK No 17
Trachsellauenen
Obersteinberg
1201
1678
1778
1792
WALK No 18
Oberhornsee
2065
N
0
1km
2km

Looking south from the Schilthorn

beyond the further one, keep left at a junction, on a wide track that rises away from the river. The climb to Gimmelwald, although never steep, maintains a steady gradient. At a little over half-way the Schiltbach brook, crossed earlier in the walk, bursts again on the scene in a spectacular waterfall.

At the first junction, if you turn right and descend slightly, passing the entrance to Gimmelwald Youth Hostel, you will come to an hotel/restaurant, strategically placed near the Gimmelwald station of the Schilthorn cableway. You can sip your coffee, or whatever, admire the superb view, and contemplate your next move – up or down in the cablecar or walking on to Mürren. If you decide on the latter, cross the road and go up a path between fences. Where it comes to a road, bear right and follow it to Mürren. Bear right in the village to the railway station.

Walk 18 Stechelberg – Trachsellauenen – Obersteinberg – Oberhornsee – Stechelberg

Map nos:	Lauterbrunnental Jungfrau Region Wanderkarte (1:33,333) Swiss Survey 264 (1:50,000) 1248 (1:25,000)
Walking time:	7 hours
Grading:	Strenuous (easy as far as Trachsellauenen). Some situations on the higher paths beyond Obersteinberg are a little exposed.
Highest altitude:	Oberhornsee 2,065m (6,775ft)
Lowest altitude:	Stechelberg 910m (2,986ft)

The spectacular Lauterbrunnen valley runs almost north–south and has an unusually level bottom between Lauterbrunnen and Stechelberg. Beyond Stechelberg the valley narrows and bends towards the south-west. High up at the valley head is the small but beautiful lake of Oberhornsee.

This walk keeps low in the valley until beyond the hotel at Trachsellauenen. Then it climbs the steep flank of the Obersteinberg passing two remote mountain hotels before the final uplift to the Oberhornsee. The return is partly along the same course but taking a higher path to Stechelberg.

You may reach the start of the walk by taking a train to Lauterbrunnen then the PTT bus for the last 6.5km to Stechelberg Hotel. The bus leaves from the terminus just outside Lauterbrunnen railway station.

The Walk

Start by walking past the hotel, going left at a fork then left again, to take the track up the left-hand side of the Tschingel Lütschine river. A fine waterfall, up to the left, sends down a stream which the track (quite wide here) crosses. At Sichellauenen, cross the second bridge over the river to gain the west bank. Where the path encounters a forestry road, turn right up it and walk round a left-hand bend before turning right to resume the original path. About 2km from Stechelberg, the small hotel at Trachsellauenen is

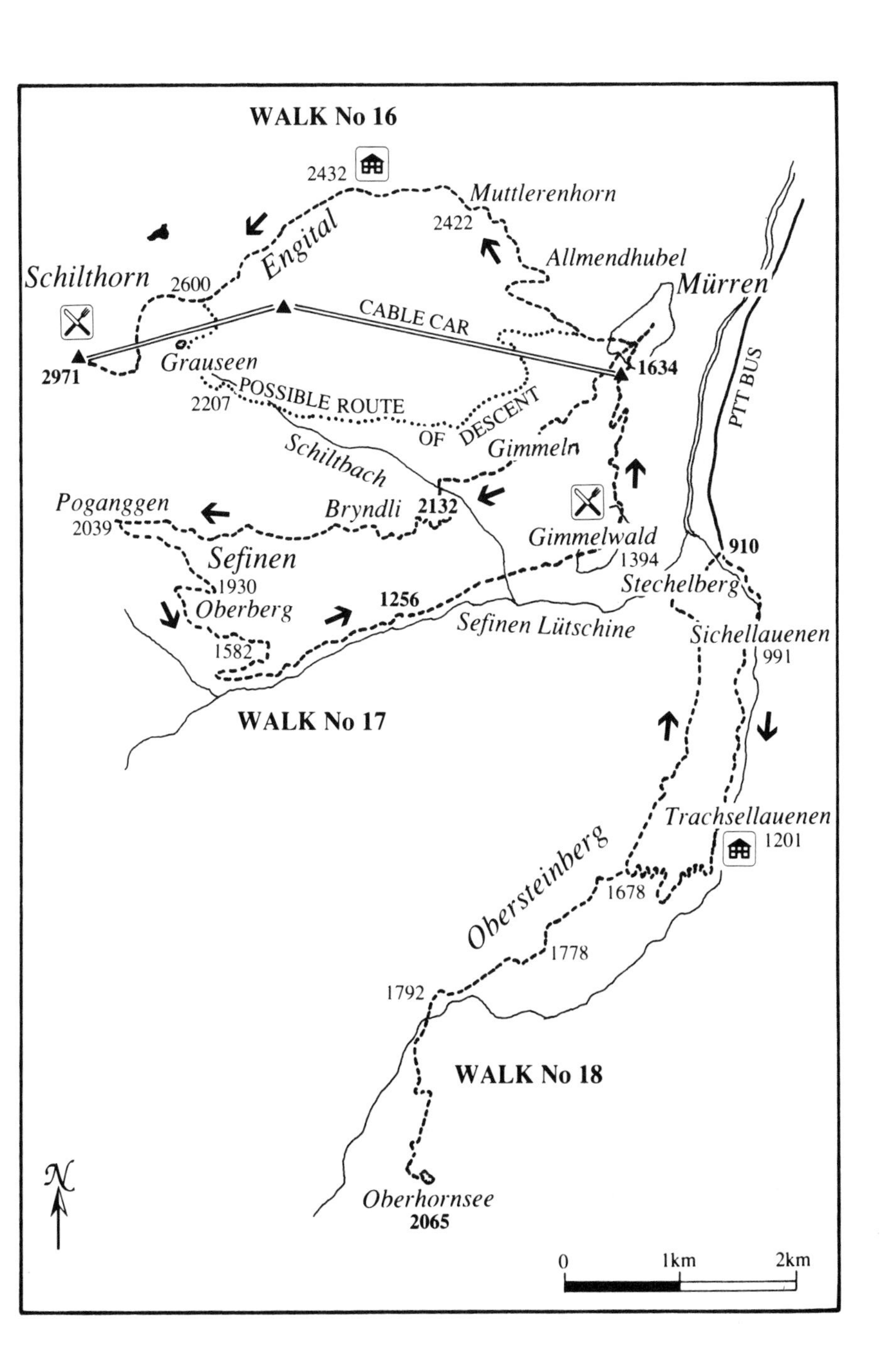
WALK No 16
2432
Muttlerenhorn
2422
Engital
Allmendhubel
Schilthorn
2600
Mürren
CABLE CAR
2971
Grauseen
1634
2207
POSSIBLE ROUTE
OF
DESCENT
PTT BUS
Schiltbach
Gimmeln
Poganggen
Bryndli
2132
2039
Gimmelwald
910
Sefinen
1394
1930
Stechelberg
Oberberg
1256
Sefinen Lütschine
Sichellauenen
1582
991
WALK No 17
Trachsellauenen
Obersteinberg
1201
1678
1778
1792
WALK No 18
N
Oberhornsee
2065
0
1km
2km

The Obersteinberg Hotel

reached (refreshments), and 0.5km further on the path splits. Take the right branch and begin to climb through the forest on what is now classified as a *Bergweg.*

Where the path emerges from the trees the views are breathtaking, with the Breithorn dominating the scene and the Schmadri Falls cascading majestically across the valley. When the path zigzags back to the right there are fine views down the Lauterbrunnen valley.

Soon after passing a cowherd's hut go left at a T-junction and very shortly you will arrive at the Tschingelhorn, a genuine mountain hotel that has *Matratzenlager* accommodation and private rooms for those wishing to stay overnight. It is a good place to sit and sip a cool drink after the climb from the valley bottom. On a sunny day the red and white umbrellas make a colourful foreground to the snowy peaks beyond.

It takes about twenty minutes to walk from the Tschingelhorn to the buildings of Obersteinberg where another mountain hotel stands (*Matratzenlager*, rooms and refreshments here also). Over this distance the path rises 100m, so the gradient is very slight. It is a path with superb views. To the left the north wall of the Oberland is crowned by a row of gleaming peaks – the Ebnefluh, Mittaghorn, Grosshorn, Breithorn and Tschingelhorn form an imposing line. Across the valley the Schmadri Falls remain a

Heading towards the peaks of Tschingelhorn and Lauterbrunnen Wetterhorn

striking feature of the landscape, and the roar of falling water is constantly in your ears.

Beyond the Obersteinberg Hotel, the path remains fairly level for a considerable distance with steep slopes to the left. At one point a landslip has made the path rather narrow and there are a few yards where the walker may feel exposed. The scenery is still magnificent, with the Lauterbrunnen Wetterhorn rising into prominence ahead. To the right the bare rocks of the Ellstabhorn tower overhead.

As the path draws near to the valley head it descends slightly towards the torrent that foams down the rocky defile. The ground has slipped locally, making the way narrow and uneven. There is a bridge over the stream but the approach can be covered in snow in early summer.

The final rise to the Oberhornsee is now seen ahead with the path slanting to the right across it. The final 60–90m (200–300ft) are perhaps the steepest of the whole route. A small lake of an almost impossible blue, the Oberhornsee is a veritable jewel set in dramatic surroundings. You can walk round it in a matter of minutes, and from almost every angle snowy summits or stern crags are reflected from its surface. The tempting waters are icy cold, even on a hot day, since it is fed by melt water from glaciers not so far away. Although the shores are rocky, the small snow gentian peeps up at you here and there.

To return, retrace your steps to the Tschingelhorn Hotel. We make no excuses for going over this ground twice, for the scenery is so lovely and on the return journey you have the Jungfrau in front. The flowers along the way are beautiful too – cornflowers, globe flowers, vetches and campion abound, and in one or two spots you may see Alpine asters. Across the valley, on the steep strips of green running up towards the crags, you can pick out the occasional cowherd's hut, highlighting the use the Swiss make of every available yard of pastureland.

Having passed the Tschingelhorn Hotel, bear left at the junction, through a gate. This path slants down and across the mountainside with sensational views into the valley below. After losing some height the tree line is reached and the path continues across and down.

Several streams and avalanche gullies are crossed, some by plank bridges. Eventually the route 'tees' into a fairly level wide path. Go left here and very soon right at another T-junction, to descend again. Soon you will see the buildings of Stechelberg below. The path ends near the Naturfreundhaus. If you bear left along a surfaced road you will shortly reach the Stechelberg Hotel and the PTT bus for the return down the valley.

Walk 19 Lauterbrunnen – Grütschalp – Mürren

Map nos:	Lauterbrunnental – Jungfrau Region Wanderkarte (1:33,333) Swiss Survey 254 & 264 (1:50,000), 1228 & 1248 (1:25,000)
Walking time:	3 hours 15 minutes
Grading:	Strenuous to Grütschalp. Easy walking from Grütschalp to Mürren. Not exposed anywhere.
Highest altitude:	Mürren 1,634m (5,361ft)
Lowest altitude:	Lauterbrunnen 795m (2,608ft)

Much of the western flank of the Lauterbrunnen valley is vertical cliff, but opposite the village the tree-clad slope leans steeply back towards Grütschalp. In 1891, a funicular railway was completed up this incline and still operates today. A footpath meanders, generally in the vicinity of the railway and forms the first part of this walk. From Grütschalp a fairly level path extends to Mürren. There is a railway here too (also opened in 1891), but this is a walk that no one should miss.

Mürren is built on the same terrace along which the path and railway run. From afar, its situation looks rather precarious, but it has become a popular summer and winter resort. It is in fact the highest permanently inhabited village in the Bernese Oberland. To the side of the main street is a monument to Sir Arnold Lunn, who was instrumental in popularising skiing as a sport, and inventor of the modern slalom.

To return to Lauterbrunnen after the walk, you can use the railway, changing at Grütschalp to the funicular, or take the cable car to Stechelberg and catch a PTT bus there. The buses connect with alternate cable cars.

The Walk

As you leave the railway station at Lauterbrunnen, cross the road and turn left. Pass the Jungfrau garage then bear right. Shortly afterwards turn right and walk up a steep path, with a stream of water in a channel to the left. Bear

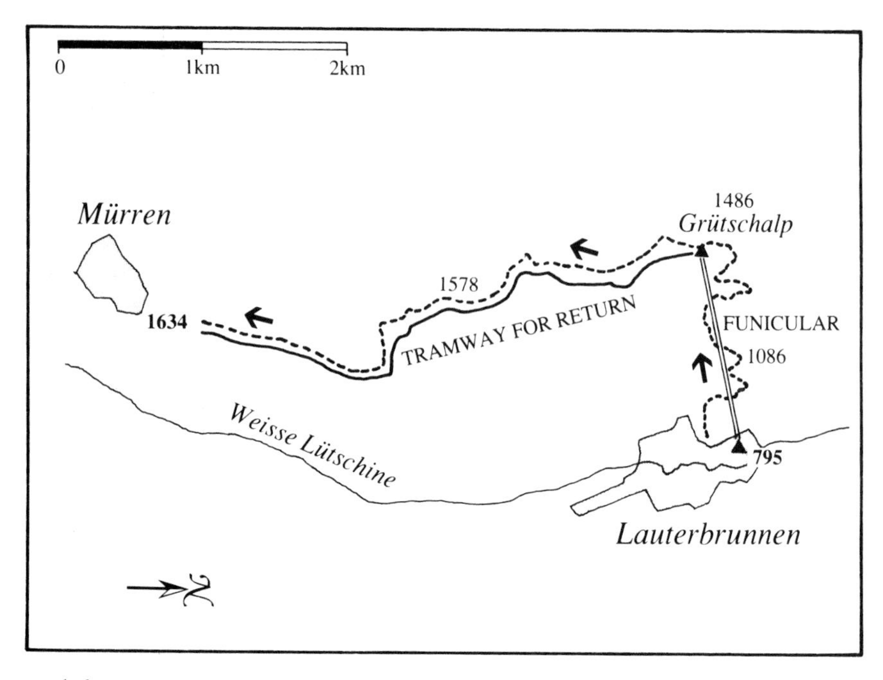

left, crossing the water, and almost immediately turn right. Go right again, re-crossing the stream and once more walk up the side of it on a path that is quite steep. Where the path veers right, ignore a branch to the left, and proceed to the funicular railway viaduct. The path goes under the railway and climbs to emerge on to a mountain road quite near a hairpin bend. Go left, round the bend, then left again before the bend is complete. Walk through a constriction and climb a grassy bank on a faint path. The path becomes better defined and slants right after a stile.

Soon you emerge on to the mountain road again in similar circumstances to those below. Turn left on the road and go partially round the bend, bearing left off it to climb a grassy bank. Go straight up it to the upper field boundary and turn left along it to enter woodland. After this the path climbs through predominantly coniferous forest. Veering left, it again goes under the railway then zigzags up quite steeply. Eventually the path veers right, under the railway for the third time and out to the mountain road.

Cross the road and proceed in the same line on a path to a T-junction. Turn left and walk again towards the line of the railway where the path bends sharply right. On reaching open ground the path bends left twice to come up to a T-junction near the line of a ski lift/chairlift. Bear left and pass along the top of Grütschalp railway station at 1,489m (4,885ft).

The Grütshalp–Mürren railway with Wengen beyond

Keep in the same line on a stony path of vehicular width. Although it rises through trees early on, the path is mostly level and proceeds through open pastureland. As you walk, the sound of cowbells will occasionally come to your ears. This typically Alpine sound is appropriate accompaniment to the feast of mountain scenery that is set before you. At first you walk with the great trio of Eiger, Mönch and Jungfrau filling your field of view. As you near Mürren the profile of the Jungfrau changes considerably, with the bare rock buttresses of the Schwarz Mönch becoming the main feature. Ahead you see a fresh array of snowy summits – Mittaghorn, Grosshorn and Breithorn.

Mürren soon comes into sight and you enter the village by the railway station. There are several places along the main street where you can sit and sip a cool drink, and contemplate the beautiful Bernese Alps.

Walk 20 Lauterbrunnen – Gsteigwiler – Wilderswil

Map nos:	Lauterbrunnental – Jungfrau Region Wanderkarte (1:33,333) Swiss Survey 254 (1:50,000), 1228 (1:25,000)
Walking time:	2 hours 30 minutes
Grading:	Easy walking. No exposure anywhere.
Highest altitude:	Lauterbrunnen 795m (2,608ft)
Lowest altitude:	Wilderswil 584m (1,916ft)

The Weisse (white) Lütschine river flows down the Lauterbrunnen valley to Zweilütschinen where it joins the Schwarz (black) Lütschine. The combined Lütschine then flows on through Wilderswil on its way to the Brienzersee (Lake Brienz).

This is a riverside walk as far as Zweilütschinen, at times right along the verge of the rushing torrent that is the Weisse Lütschine. After crossing the Schwarz Lütschine the route gradually veers away from the river bank and becomes a forest walk above Gsteigwiler. It then descends to this village and continues through meadow and wood to return to the Lütschine at Wilderswil.

The Walk

Emerging from Lauterbrunnen railway station go right and soon you will see Hotel/Restaurant Sternen on the right. Bear right immediately after the building, pass under the railway, and straight away go left on a path that soon descends towards the river. Shortly the path crosses the torrent by means of a substantial girder bridge and hugs the right bank to the hamlet of Lochbrucke.

Walk between the buildings on what is now a surfaced road, and, where the road swings right, bear left back to the river bank. For a time the route alternates between stony track and pleasant walking on grass, sometimes at the water's edge. The river itself is a dramatic spectacle as it crashes its tumultuous way over boulders of all sizes and indulges in a low waterfall at one point.

Where the path reaches a fairly wide track, bear left with cliffs now

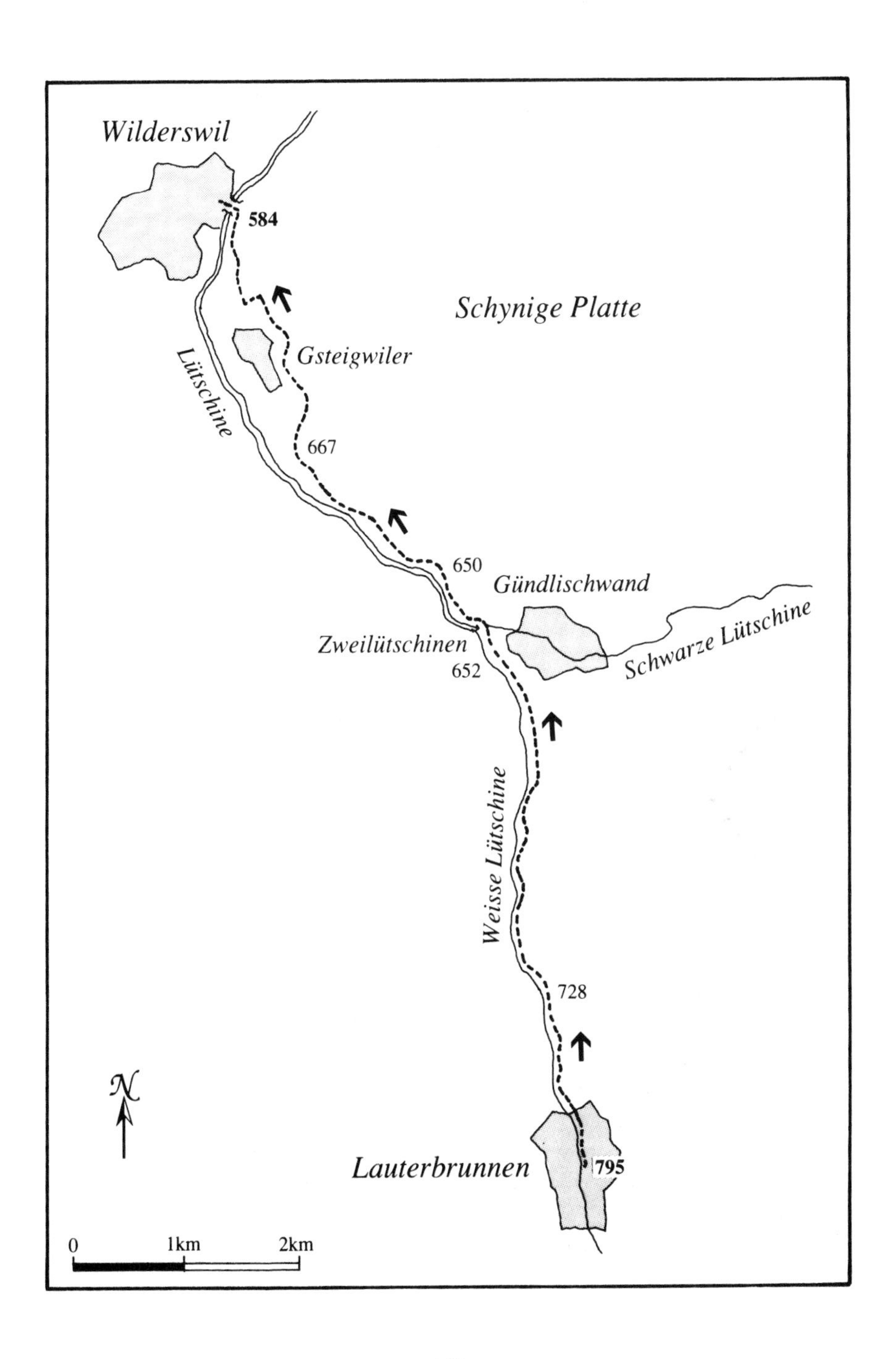
Wilderswil
584
Schynige Platte
Gsteigwiler
Lütschine
667
650
Gündlischwand
Zweilütschinen
652
Schwarze Lütschine
Weisse Lütschine
728
N
Lauterbrunnen
795
0
1km
2km

The old church of Gsteig near Wilderswil

towering above on the other side of the river. The heights of Schynige Platte loom ahead as you walk. To the left of the track are the remains of an old furnace, massively built but now becoming progressively vegetated. Presently you will come down to the railway and the village of Zweilütschinen will appear. Cross the road and walk down to and through the railway station. Just beyond go right, over a level crossing, then left to follow the rails to the crossing of the Schwarz Lütschine. There is a pedestrian way just to the right of the railway bridge, and you can see to the left the confluence of the Weisse and the Schwarz Lütschine rivers. 'Schwarz' (black) would seem to be an overstatement; it is, perhaps, a shade or two of grey darker than its 'white' counterpart.

The (quite wide) path now follows the railway then draws away to the right, rising through agricultural land. Looking back you can see the summit of the Mönch with the Jungfraujoch to the right and the nearer Männlichen in front. At a junction bear right on a road that continues to climb with a heliport to the right. As it levels out you walk with dense beech woods sloping up to the right.

Where the road begins to descend, go left to the chalets of Gsteigwiler. Turn right along a path between fences and, passing a point where Wilderswil can be seen below, descend through a wood. A level path with bushes to the left brings you to the Schynige Platte railway line. Cross this and take a path through trees. Go straight over a cross-track and descend through a beech wood to a road. The river can now be seen below with the houses of Wilderswil beyond.

Go down the road to the church of Gsteig passing the picturesque Steinbok Inn, believed to have been built in 1797. The church dates back to 1133, although it has been extensively restored. Its most obvious feature is the Baroque tower but there are parts of Gothic and Roman origin. Below the church, cross the quaint covered Gsteig bridge, built in 1738. Of the three roads opposite, take the middle one to the railway station, where you can get a train back to Lauterbrunnen if you have to return to that resort.

Walk 21 Wengen – Männlichen – Kleine Scheidegg – Wengernalp – Wengen

Map nos:	Lauterbrunnental – Jungfrau Region Wanderkarte (1:33,333) Swiss Survey 254 (1:50,000), 1228 & 1229 (1:25,000)
Walking time:	7 hours 30 minutes
Grading:	Fairly strenuous over the ascent of the Männlichen, moderately exposed in one or two places. The rest is safe, easy walking.
Highest altitude:	Summit of Männlichen 2,343m (7,686ft)
Lowest altitude:	Wengen 1,274m (4,180ft)

From the Eiger a great spur thrusts north-west, dividing the Lütschental from the Lauterbrunnental. The Männlichen is the final peak of the ridge, overlooking the meeting of these two valleys. From Wengen, situated on a shelf above the Lauterbrunnen valley, the path to the summit of the Männlichen is for most of the ascent steep and narrow. By contrast the way from Männlichen to Kleine Scheidegg is comfortably wide and easy, crossing a vast mountainside. The track down from Kleine Scheidegg is wide and stony but narrows as the surroundings become more pastoral beyond Wengernalp. As you get nearer to Wengen the way becomes a road of easy gradient.

It is possible to shorten the walk in several ways, if desired. You may miss out the climb to the Männlichen by taking the cable car from Wengen, or you can return to Wengen by railway from Kleine Scheidegg or Wengernalp.

The Walk

Taking Wengen's railway station as the starting point, walk up the approach road and turn left into the main street. Go as far as the Hotel Bernerhof and bear right on a surfaced path. Walk past the English church to the Park Hotel and just afterwards bear left up a stony track. At a junction take the left fork (signposted Leiterhorn) soon passing between wooden huts. On reaching a T-junction turn left and walk to the huts of Aussere Allmend, where you bear right on a lesser path. Where this joins a wide track go right, and just after a left-hand bend bear right on a path that ascends steeply between trees. Climb steadily through forestry by way of numerous zigzags. On emerging on to open mountainside you will find yourself on a climbing traverse that slants to the right. There are steep slopes below to your right hand as you look down on to the villages of Lauterbrunnen and Wengen.

Across the valley the peak of the Bietenhorn is a prominent feature, and to its right is the strange rock tooth of the Lobhorner. Alpine flowers make a colourful show, with wild pansies prolific from May to July.

Where the path reaches a junction, go left and start to zigzag upwards again. The summit of the Mönch appears above the skyline of the Männlichen ridge only to slide from view again, but it is soon back and, within a few yards, the peak of the Eiger can be seen as well. Soon the path slants right again, towards the buildings near the top of the cableway. There is a feeling of exposure here in one or two spots, for the path is narrow and the slopes to the right quite steep, but there is nothing to bother anyone with a reasonably steady head. When the path reaches the line of the cableway a few more zigzags take you to the top of the ridge near the cable car station.

The summit of the Männlichen is now 20 minutes away to the left, most of it on a surfaced path. Having gone so far, who would shirk going on to the top? The walk is well worth taking, for the view from this lofty perch is superb. Not only do the Oberland giants stand in line to the south (Wetterhorn, Schreckhorn, Eiger, Mönch, Jungfrau, Breithorn, Tschingelhorn and Gspaltenhorn, from left to right), the northern skyline from Schynige Platte to the Schwarzhorn catches the eye across the deep trench of the Lütschental. To the west is a sea of peaks, too many to name individually, and there is a glimpse of the Thunnersee to the north-west.

You turn reluctantly from this grand viewpoint, but from now on it is virtually downhill all the way. Retrace your steps to the cable car station and advance towards the terminus of the Grindelwald–Männlichen gondola cableway (at 6.2km, the longest gondola cableway in Europe). Among the complex of buildings here is a well-equipped restaurant. You might like to stay a while for refreshment, or even a meal, but before you leave go over to a viewpoint to the right to enjoy the views into the Lauterbrunnen valley. Then head south following signs to Kleine Scheidegg. Take the right fork after a short distance, and follow this delightful path as it rounds the great bulk of the Tschuggen, losing height slowly but steadily. At one point it swings right, giving you a striking profile of the Lauberhorn as you descend

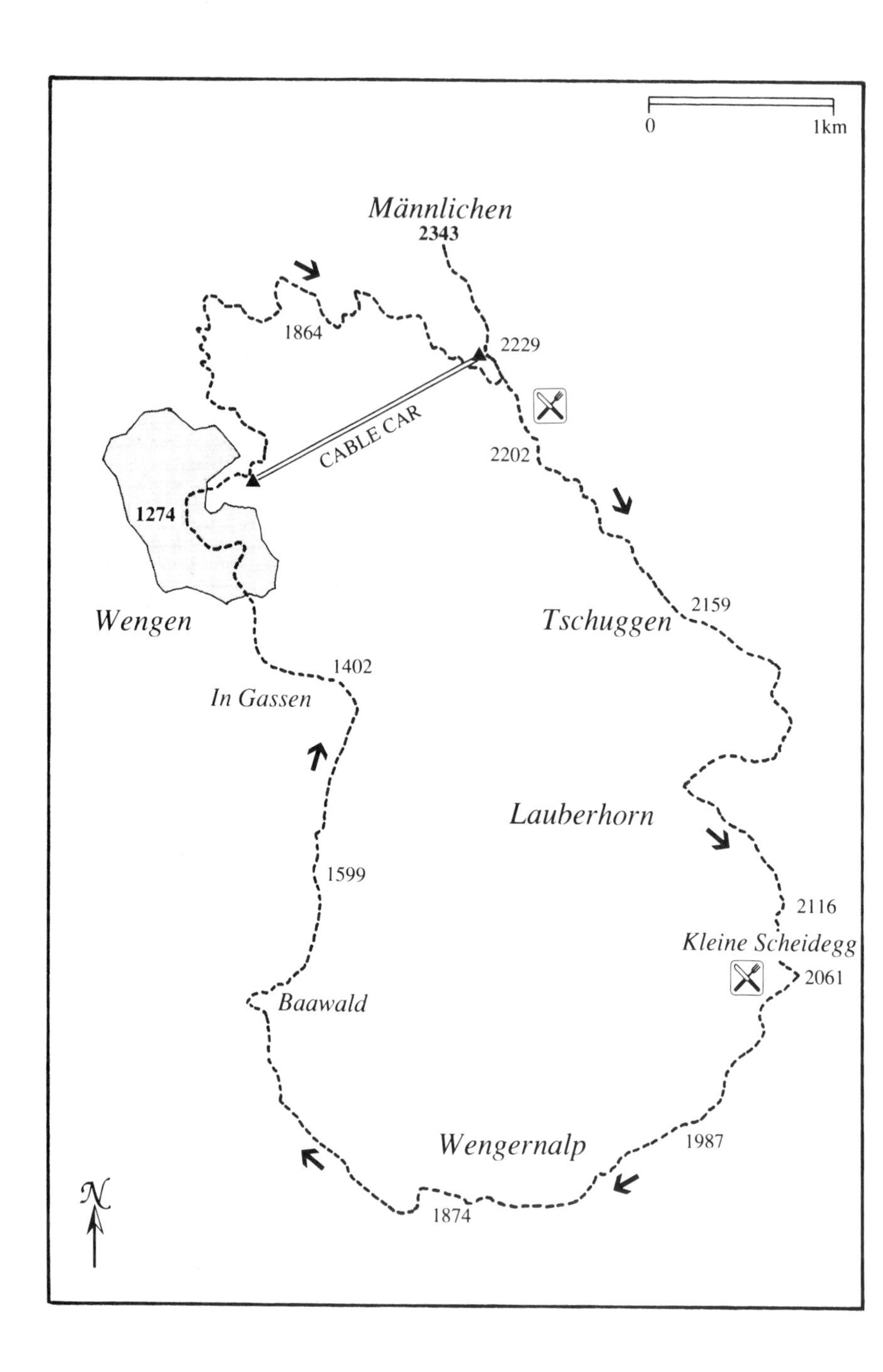
0
1km
Männlichen
2343
1864
2229
CABLE CAR
2202
1274
Wengen
Tschuggen
2159
1402
In Gassen
Lauberhorn
1599
2116
Kleine Scheidegg
2061
Baawald
Wengernalp
1987
1874
N

The Männlichen-Grindelwald cableway below the Tschuggen

towards a stream. The path turns left again and soon you can see the buildings of Kleine Scheidegg below.

Kleine Scheidegg itself does not match the wonderful scenery that surrounds it. Its buildings are anything but beautiful and it's usually thronged with people, most of whom have arrived there by train. However, if it's refreshment that you're looking for, then you will find it in plenty. There are eating places here to suit every taste, as well as the ubiquitous souvenir shops. The dominating feature visible from Kleine Scheidegg is, of course, the great north face of the Eiger – the famous Nordwand. This was the place from which the early attempts on the face were followed through telescopes. It was also the base from which many of the climbers set out, some never to return.

From near the railway station a broad track descends, south-westerly (signposted 'Wengernalp und Wengen'), following the same course as the railway and keeping just below it. To the left across the valley is the vast complicated side of the Jungfrau. If you hear a rumble, look across and see if you can spot the snow or ice tumbling down; on a hot afternoon you may see several such falls.

Just before reaching Wengernalp station the track goes under the railway to continue on the upper side. Beyond the station turn left from the main track, back under the railway track. At first this path keeps close to the rails but then it gradually draws away from them and descends over pleasant grassy Alpine meadows. Keep on down, ignoring a turning to the left, until the path comes to a broad stony road. Bear right along it and follow it until it joins the main track from Wengernalp.

Bear left and walk towards Wengen with picturesque chalets becoming ever more numerous to either side, their balconies and gardens bright with flowers. In the village go under the railway, turn left and walk down to the station.

Walk 22 Wengen – Leiterhorn – Spätenalp – Burglauenen – Grindelwald

Map nos:	Lauterbrunnental – Jungfrau Region Wanderkarte (1:33,333) Swiss Survey 254 (1:50,000), 1228 & 1229 (1:25,000)
Walking time:	4 hours 30 minutes
Grading:	Moderate. There are situations between Spätenalp and Burglauenen that are a little exposed.
Highest altitude:	Spätenalp 1,553m (5,095ft)
Lowest altitude:	Burglauenen 893m (2,930ft)

The Leiterhorn is a viewpoint north of Wengen above the junction of two valleys; the Lütschental descending west from Grindelwald and the Lauterbrunnental descending towards the north. It is reached on an easy path from Wengen in about $1^{1}/_{4}$ hours. Thereafter the route takes a fairly level course to Spätenalp, where a descending traverse is begun towards Burglauenen. This latter section is classed as a *Bergweg* and there are places where a steady head is an advantage. Finally, you walk along the bank of the Schwarz Lütschine river to Schwendi, before climbing up the north flank of the valley and descending into Grindelwald. The walk can be cut short at Burglauenen or Schwendi and a train taken back down valley or on to Grindelwald.

The Walk

Walk away from Wengen railway station and turn left into the main street. Go past the Hotel Bernerhof and then turn left to walk past the Hotels Belvedere and Alpenruhe. Opposite a small timber store turn right and you will soon come to a small clearing with a row of huts where you keep straight on through a gate. Soon you will find yourself climbing a path with, when looking back, unrivalled views of the Lauterbrunnen valley.

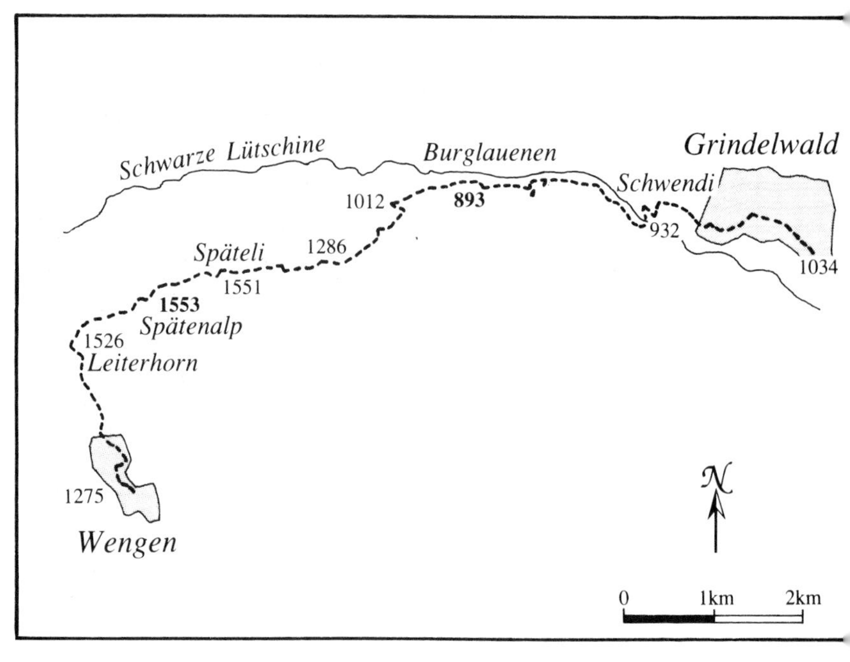

Bear right by a hay loft and turn left by a signpost (direction Leiterhorn, Spätenalp, Burglauenen). Where the path reaches the corner of a wooded area turn right and climb, parallel with the edge of the forestry, on a stepped path. Where the gradient eases a signpost directs the visitor leftwards through the trees to the Leiterhorn viewpoint, only a few minutes away (1,525m, 5,003ft).

The view from here is largely a northerly one but, although none of the big Oberland peaks are included, it is still an impressive panorama. Straight in front and at a great depth is the lower part of the Lütschinen valley. Seemingly at your feet can be seen Zweilütschinen and, further away,the villages of Gsteigwiler and Wilderswil. Across the valley to the left you can pick out the small village of Isenfluh while in front and extending rightwards is an impressive group of mountains. From the group of peaks round Schynige Platte the eye wanders over the Loucherhorn, Ussri, Indri, the Faulhorn and Reeti.

Having feasted your eyes on this vast landscape retrace your steps to the signpost where you bear left to a further signpost. Go left into the forest and join up with a forestry road. Keep left where the forestry road swings right and follow an undulating path. Soon after leaving the trees the Wetterhorn appears in front. Presently you will see the chalet of Spätenalp ahead and just

The Lauterbrunnen valley from above Wengen

before reaching it turn left downhill. The route now becomes classified as a *Bergweg* and, although the path is narrow, the way is generously embellished with white/red/white flashes.

Before entering the forest you may see the *Alpenrose* growing on the slopes near the path. After descending through trees the route becomes a horizontal traverse and crosses several avalanche gullies. In one or two of these, snow can persist well into the summer season. Some have log platforms constructed to make the crossings safer, but since most of these gullies are quite steep there is an element of exposure. Eventually the path begins to climb again, zigzagging up through dense woodland, then it levels out, with steep slopes to the left.

The trees thin out and the path descends past the chalet of Ritten. Another wooded area follows, then you descend on a much wider path with fresh views of the Wetterhorn up valley. At a junction turn sharply left and soon bend right. The way becomes a surfaced road descending past the occasional chalet residence. In the valley bottom it crosses the Schwarz Lütschine with Burglauenen railway station a little beyond.

Turn right just before the river bridge and walk on a surfaced path past farm buildings with the Wetterhorn straight ahead. The tarmac comes to an end by the last inhabited building and presently the path bends left to the river

On the path between Leiterhorn and Spätenalp

and continues along the bank. A complex of buildings appears ahead and the path becomes surfaced again. Turn left over a bridge and pass Schwendi railway station. Emerging on to the main road, walk along it to the right as far as the Schweizerheim Restaurant, where you turn left. The path upwards is quite steep but the torrent on the left may have a cooling influence if the day is warm. When confronted by a stone wall go right and emerge into the open with grassy slopes on either side.

Continue in the same line and the way becomes a road that ascends between attractive residential chalets. At a crossroads turn right and descend into Grindelwald village, known as the glacier village because of its proximity to the Unter-Grindelwald glacier. Grindelwald is dominated by the Wetterhorn to the east and the Eiger to the south. In between them the Mättenberg presents a craggy face towards the valley.

If you intend to return to Wengen or Lauterbrunnen by train it is far less expensive to travel via Zweilütschinen than to go by way of Kleine Scheidegg.

Walk 23 Wengen – Staubachbankli – Staldenfluh – Brechalp – Trümmelbach – Lauterbrunnen

Map nos:	Lauterbrunnental – Jungfrau Region Wanderkarte (1:33,333) Swiss Survey 254 & 264 (1:50,000), 1228 & 1248 (1:25,000)
Walking time:	4 hours 45 minutes
Grading:	Easy walking to Staubachbankli and from Trümmelbach to Lauterbrunnen. The remainder is moderate, but in some places between Brechalp and Trümmelbach there is a degree of exposure, especially the final 30m or so of descent.
Highest altitude:	Staldenboden 1,670m (5,479ft)
Lowest altitude:	Lauterbrunnen 790m (2,592ft)

This varied walk takes you first to Staubachbankli, a popular viewpoint, then through Ronen Forest ascending to Staldenfluh, another viewpoint. The path becomes a *Bergweg* as the route descends, first to Brechalp, then further to cross the Trümmelbach stream. The final descent into the Lauterbrunnen valley is over increasingly steep ground, which, although protected, needs a steady head. At the bottom, you are quite near to the Trümmelbach Falls from where the route goes down valley, including some riverside walking to Lauterbrunnen. It is possible to cut the walk short by catching the PTT bus to Lauterbrunnen, at Trümmelbach.

The Walk

From Wengen railway station walk up the road by the side of the railway and go right, through the underpass. Proceed in the direction of Kleine Scheidegg for perhaps 300m and bear right by a house named 'Beaulieu'. Where this path levels out there are good views of Wengen to the right. Straight ahead, the village of Mürren can be seen in its incredible situation, on the edge of

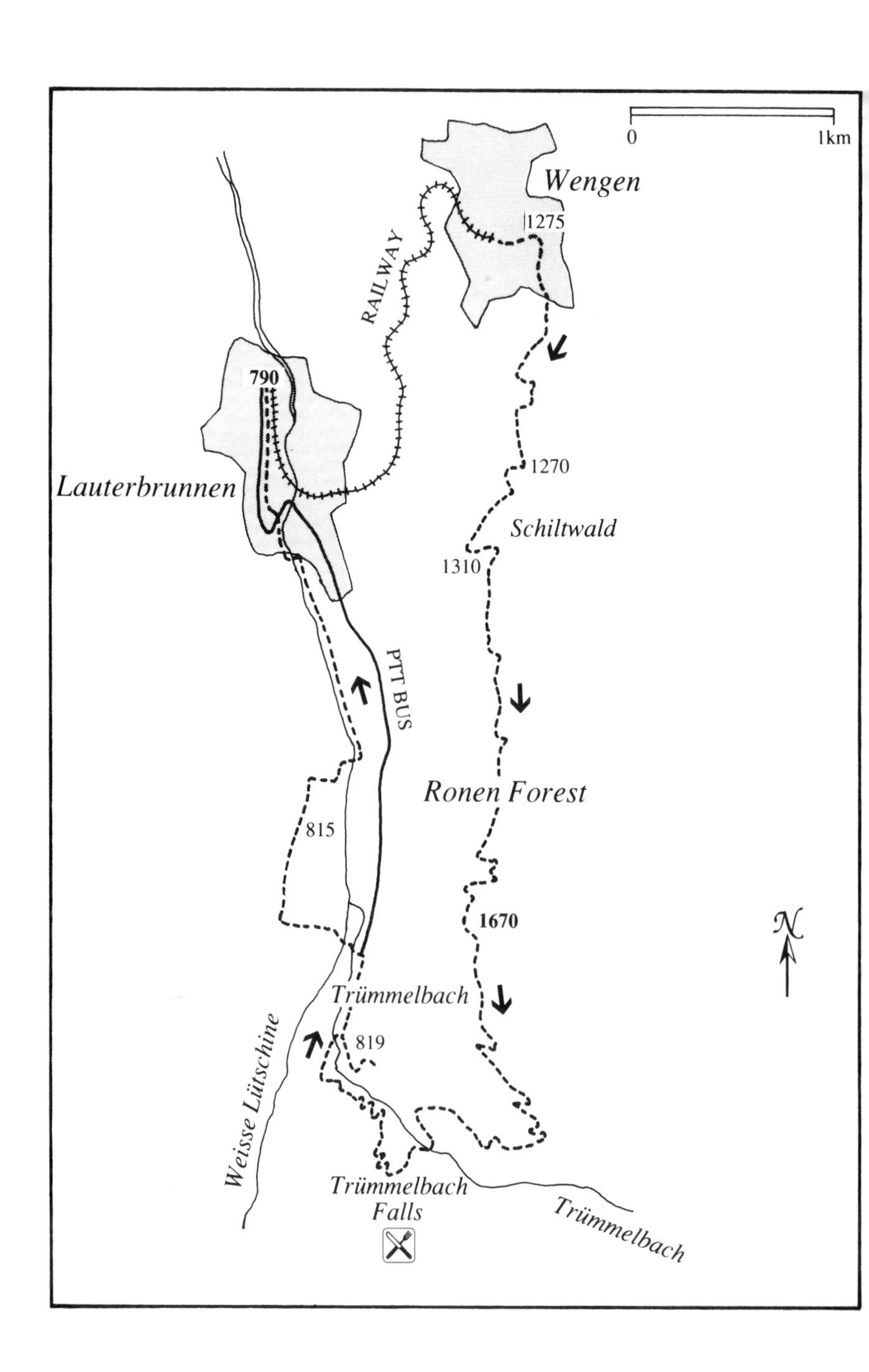
0
1km
Wengen
1275
RAILWAY
790
Lauterbrunnen
1270
Schiltwald
1310
PTT BUS
Ronen Forest
815
1670
N
Trümmelbach
819
Weisse Lütschine
Trümmelbach
Falls
Trümmelbach

a precipice. At a cross-paths keep straight on and descend past a tree with seats round it. The path is stepped here and continues steeply down between trees. Where it joins a road, bear left on a bridge over a stream. Follow the road round, past Mary's Café (refreshments) and keep right at a junction to the viewpoint of Staubachbankli (altitude 1,276m, 4,186ft).

The first thing you notice here is the number of seats – you should have no difficulty finding somewhere to rest your legs. Stand, however, for a while, and savour the view of the Lauterbrunnen valley far below, with the main feature, the Staubach waterfall, on the opposite side. A spout of water leaps out at the top of the cliff and falls 300m (about 1,000ft) clear of the rock. To the left and only slightly less spectacular is the fall of the Spissbach.

To resume the walk, face away from the viewpoint and walk steeply up for perhaps 200m, past chalets. At a T-junction at the top turn right and for a time walk comfortably on a level path. Having entered the forest of Ronen the paths starts to climb and continues upwards with zigzags in places.

Eventually, the viewpoint of Staldenfluh (altitude 1,600m, 5,249ft) is reached and here the feeling of remoteness from the valley bottom is even more pronounced than at Staubachbankli. The gulf below is 800m (2,600ft). Seats have been provided here at a series of different levels.

The path climbs on for a short distance to a junction at the edge of the trees. Bear right and almost immediately begin to descend. About half an hour from the junction, pass the chalet at Brechalp and below this descend towards the Trümmel valley, with two fine waterfalls pouring off the Jungfrau straight ahead. You will now be very aware of the Trümmelbach stream as it thunders down the defile below. The path since the junction is designated as a *Bergweg* (marked with white/red/white flashes), and the reason for this becomes clear as the mountainside steepens. However, where there is some exposure, handrails have been provided and at one place a whole metal staircase has been installed. The path zigzags down, maintaining a general direction roughly parallel to the Trümmelbach, and then, where the gradient relents, it moves left and descends to a footbridge. Pause here to enjoy the situation. The torrent pours down the defile in a series of cascades and almost immediately under the bridge plunges in a sizeable waterfall, before disappearing between water-worn walls of rock.

Beyond the bridge you have to scramble out of the gorge. The path zigzags steeply up with wire cables in places to provide assistance. Once up, the route moves away from the Trümmelbach before descending again down a slope that becomes increasingly steeper. There are many zigzags and they continue over the thirty metres or so where the path is down solid rock. Again, safety cables are in place here.

The descent finishes by the Trümmelbach as it emerges from the rock wall, the final cascade of the series crashing down to the right. The route crosses a level meadow to the valley road where you turn right to pass the entrance to the Trümmelbach Falls complex. There is a restaurant and a souvenir shop here, and if you have time the falls themselves are worth a visit. The entrance fee is SFr 6, which entitles the visitor to make the ascent in a giant lift and then to explore the concrete walkways. These allow you to see the impressive cascades at close quarters, most of them deep into the mountain itself and beautifully illuminated. There is a feeling of frightening power here, perhaps not surprising, since the Trümmelbach drains the glaciers of the Jungfrau, Mönch and Eiger and the flow can be up to 20,000 litres (4,500 gallons) per second.

From outside the restaurant it is possible to get a PTT bus to Lauterbrunnen. They call at Trümmelbach at about $^{1}/_{4}$ to the hour (last one at 6.45pm).

If you prefer to walk, proceed along the road for 300m or so and turn left on a path that goes over a river bridge. Cross the valley floor to a narrow road where you turn right for almost half a mile. Go right to cross the Weisse Lütschine then go left along the river bank, passing the heliport. After re-crossing the river, the path emerges on to the road by the church. Almost opposite, a further path leads up to the main street of Lauterbrunnen. Go right to reach the railway station, where you can get a train back to Wengen, if required.

Walk 24 Männlichen – Bustiglen – Grindelwald

Map nos:	Lauterbrunnental – Jungfrau Region Wanderkarte (1:33,333) Swiss Survey 254 (1:50,000), 1229 (1:25,000)
Walking time:	3 hours 30 minutes
Grading:	Easy walking. No exposure anywhere.
Highest altitude:	Männlichen Cableway Station 2,229m (7,313ft)
Lowest altitude:	Grindelwald Grund 943m (3,094ft)

To reach the start of this walk you can ride up from Wengen by cable car (8 minutes and costs SFr 14.40) or take a gondola (30 minutes and SFr 20) from Grindelwald. (Either fare subject to 50 per cent discount to Half Fare Travel Card holders.) You could of course walk up from Wengen (*see* Walk 21), adding three hours to the walking time.

The route first traverses open mountainside to Bustiglen then becomes a woodland walk through the Forest of Itramenwald before descending through meadowland to Grund. The final part up to Grindelwald is through an urban area and you may prefer to take the train, saving 25 minutes of walking time.

The Walk

Having arrived at the cable car station , you may want to visit the summit of the Männlichen. Allow 35 minutes, there and back, plus viewing time. This might be appreciable because it is a fine viewpoint.

The scenery from the cable car station itself is quite breathtaking, the dark mass of the Tschuggen making a fine foreground to the glories of the Jungfrau behind. Looking across the gulf of the Lauterbrunnen valley the summits of the Bietenhorn, Schilthorn, Gspaltenhorn and Blümlisalp can be picked out.

From the cable car station walk towards Kleine Scheidegg but take the left fork where the ways divide. This path is classed as a *Bergweg*, but is always well-defined and the walking is easy and safe. It traverses the open mountainside of Tschuggen's flank, losing height all the way, although sometimes it is

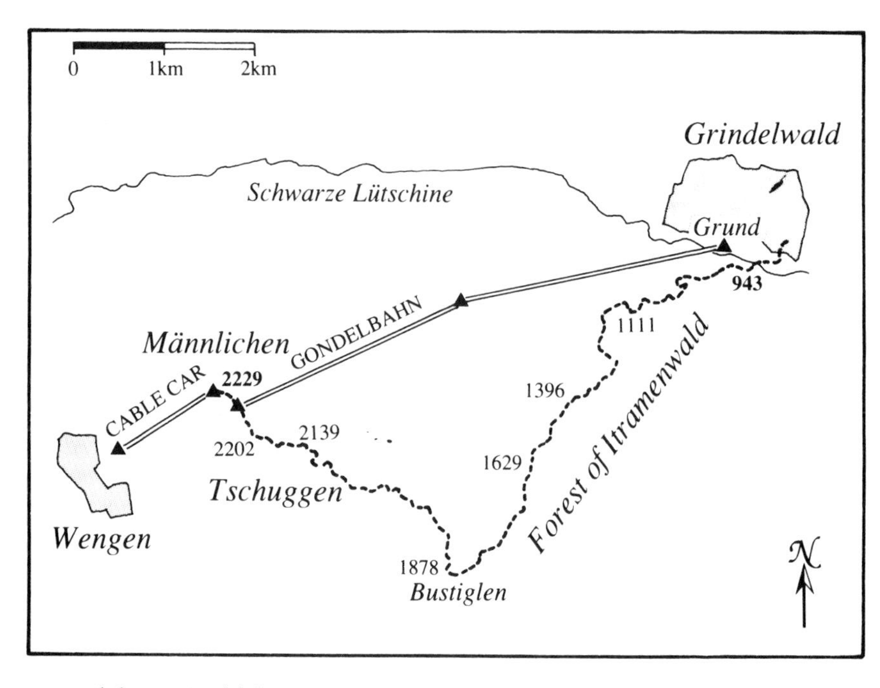

undulating. Wild flowers abound, especially in early summer when you will see pansies, crocuses and anemones. Over one section the trumpet gentian outnumbers everything else. The Eiger dominates the landscape, becoming more commanding as you walk towards it; the Jungfrau and the Mönch are also prominent, and the Wetterhorn too, as the path meanders delightfully.

At a junction bear right on a track that takes you towards a group of chalets and huts. This is Bustiglen (altitude 1,878m, 6,161ft) where looking right, you can see the hotels of Kleine Scheidegg on the top of the pass. Straight ahead, the much-used track from Kleine Scheidegg to Alpiglen stands out like a scar across the lower slopes of the Eiger. Turn left at a four-way junction and descend on a narrow path. Over open ground at first, the path soon enters Itramenwald forest where it winds amongst the dense trees. The principal hazard is tripping over tree roots.

A kilometre from the junction you pass along the shore of a delightful forest pool and after a further kilometre another larger pool appears through the trees to the left; this might make an excellent picnic spot.

After another 200m, take the right branch at a forked junction and begin to descend more steeply. Go straight over a four-way junction and on to a 'tee' with a stony forest road. Go right and almost immediately left on a road of similar width. This road bends to the right and, having walked round the bend, go left on a narrow path. Descend through dense trees to emerge on to meadowland. Grindelwald can now be seen below with the Wetterhorn and the great wall of the Mättenberg in the right background. Where the path gives on to a road of vehicular width follow this down to a motor road. Turn right and follow the road as it bends left, then go right again down a path between fences. The path narrows before again joining the motor road where you turn right. Walk along the road (which is fairly level here) until just beyond the Restaurant Aspen.

Go left and shortly bear right by a ski lift on a path that descends near a stream. The path widens and after two hairpin bends comes to a motor road. Turn right along it and walk past the Eiger Nordwand Campsite.

Soon you can bear left across the Schwarz Lütschine river to Grund railway station. Some may prefer to take a train up to the centre of Grindelwald; they run about every half -hour during the summer season.

To finish the walk under your own power, bear right and walk up the road beside the railway line. The railway veers away to the left but you follow the road through until it joins the main street of Grindelwald. Turn left for the railway station. If you intend to return to Wengen or Lauterbrunnen by train, it is far less expensive to travel via Zweilütschinen than to go by way of Kleine Scheidegg.

Walk 25 Grindelwald – Halsegg – Pfingstegg – Mamorbruch – Grindelwald

Map nos:	Wanderkarte Berner Oberland Ost (1:50,000) Swiss Survey 254 (1:50,000), 1229 (1:25,000)
Walking time:	3 hours 45 minutes (not including time taken in walking to and from the ice grotto or in visiting the upper glacier)
Grading:	Easy walking. No exposure anywhere.
Highest altitude:	Pfingstegg 1,392m (4,567ft)
Lowest altitude:	Bridge near the Gletscherdorf Campsite, 989m (3,245ft)

Facing Grindelwald across the valley of the Schwarz Lütschine is the massive bulk of the Mättenberg, which is really a spur of the Schreckhorn. To the left of it, as seen from Grindelwald, the snout of the Oberer Grindelwald Glacier protrudes through the gap confined on the other side by the Wetterhorn.

This walk descends to cross the Schwarz Lütschine then ascends through woodland to Halsegg with the opportunity of visiting the glacier. The route then traverses across the steep slopes of the Mättenberg, passing Pfingstegg before descending to the Mamorbruch Restaurant and on to Grindelwald. The walk may be shortened by descending from Pfingstegg by cable car.

The Walk

Emerging from Grindelwald railway station, walk eastwards along the main street. Turn right just before the Sunstar Hotel and follow the narrow road down and round to the left until it joins a wider road. Turn right and go down to the Schwarz Lütschine river, cross the bridge and immediately turn left. Walk along the river bank at first, with the Wetterhorn towering ahead. Then the narrow road climbs away from the river passing a number of houses. As it swings right, fork left and shortly draw close to the river again.

Soon, bear right on a path that rises through woodland. Keep left at a

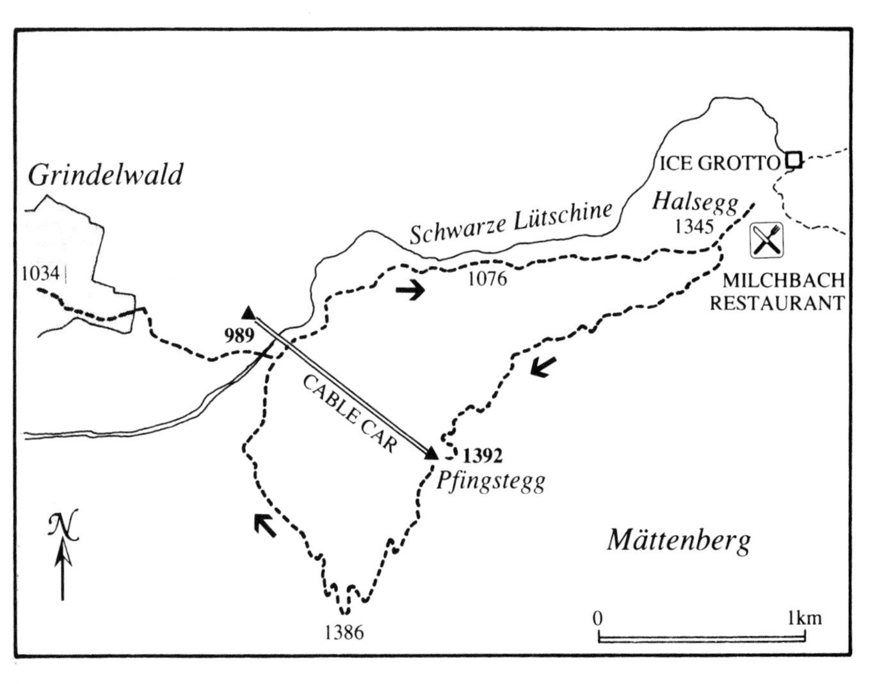

junction and after 0.8km, when faced with a wall of rock, zigzag up the steep slope with the rock to your left-hand side.

At a T-junction go left and walk for about 10 minutes to the Restaurant Milchbach at 1,348m (4,423ft). This is Halsegg, and having emerged from the forest you can now see the snout of the Oberer Grindelwald Glacier in its cleft between the Wetterhorn and the Mättenberg. Here you can descend a path to visit an ice grotto in the bottom edge of the glacier, visit the upper glacier or go into the restaurant.

The ice grotto is a short downhill walk away. One notice says 10 minutes, another says 5. In practice it is something between the two. Walking back up again takes slightly longer. Having walked down you will first come to a souvenir stall and, beyond it, the grotto. Admittance is SFr 3 each. It provides a novel experience, although it is an advantage to have a waterproof with you, as drips are constantly falling from the roof. The ice cave winds slightly, so you are soon out of sight of the entrance, and there is an unearthly blue glow. At the end, electric lights illuminate ice carvings and.there is an inner sanctum with log seats.

The visit to the upper glacier surface also costs SFr 3 and includes the use of a prepared way from the restaurant that ascends over rocks, using ladders in places. This is taken at your own risk, of course.

The snout of the Oberer Grindelwald Glacier

When you are ready to leave, go back along the path to the T-junction, but now keep left. The route crosses the mountainside, maintaining a generally level course, with forest below and the beetling crags of the Mättenberg above. Several watercourses are passed. One that is only a trickle in dry conditions can present some difficulty when the weather is wet. Another in a ravine is crossed by a footbridge. Ignore two branches to the right and you will arrive at the upper station of the Grindelwald–Pfingstegg cableway which was opened in 1967. The station incorporates a restaurant (refreshments).

Keep on the same path, past some rocks and over another stream that is likely to give you wet feet if it is, or has been, raining. In 10–15 minutes from Pfingstegg, turn sharply right and descend. Soon turn left on a *Bergweg* that goes down through woodland, with zigzags here and there, to the Mamorbruch Restaurant (refreshments). Passing to the left of the building, turn right, round the corner of it, then at the corner of the car park go left on a path. This descends through trees to the motor road that comes from the car park. (You can turn left down the road, then left again to visit the Gletscherlucht, a gorge formed by ice and water from the Unterer Grindelwald Glacier.)

Go straight over on to a path that descends at first through woodland then over open ground to a level motor road. Turn right and walk along the road to the bridge over the Schwarz Lütschine that you crossed early in the walk. Re-cross it and retrace your steps up the hill to Grindelwald.

Walk 26 Brienzer Rothorn – Arnihaaggen – Brünig Pass

Map nos:	Oberhasli Wanderkarte (1:50,000) Swiss Survey 254 (1:50,000), 1209 (1:25,000)
Walking time:	4 hours 30 minutes
Grading:	Moderate. Mild exposure in one or two places.
Highest altitude:	Rothorn summit 2,350m (7,707ft)
Lowest altitude:	Just below Brünig Pass 990m (3,248ft)

The Rothorn rises to the north of the town of Brienz from where a 'cogwheel' railway ascends almost to the summit. The Brienzer Rothorn Bahn, to give it its official name, was one of the earliest mountain railways in the Alps (1892) and still retains a number of the original steam engines, although there are now some diesel ones as well. The journey from Brienz to the upper station takes 55 minutes.

From the Rothorn, a ridge that includes several other lesser summits descends a little south of eastwards, towards the Brünig Pass. The walk starts from the summit station and follows the ridge for a while, then leaving it descends on the south side via Wileralp to the Brünig Pass. From here it is possible to return to Brienz by rail, via Meiringen.

The Walk

From the Brienzer Rothorn Bahn station (restaurant) walk up to the summit passing the upper station of the Schonenboden cableway (restaurant). This is a favourite starting place for paragliders, so you are quite likely to see these sportsmen at close quarters. The view from the top, as you might guess, is superb. However, the high Oberland peaks are only seen above the intervening mountain mass, of which the Schwarzhorn is the highest. Above this appear the snowy summits of Wellhorn, Wetterhorn, Schreckhorn, Finsteraarhorn, Eiger, Mönch and Jungfrau, the latter from this angle having a more pointed summit than in the usual profile seen from other places. To the right of these are Breithorn, Tschingelhorn, Gspaltenhorn and the Blümlisalp. Further

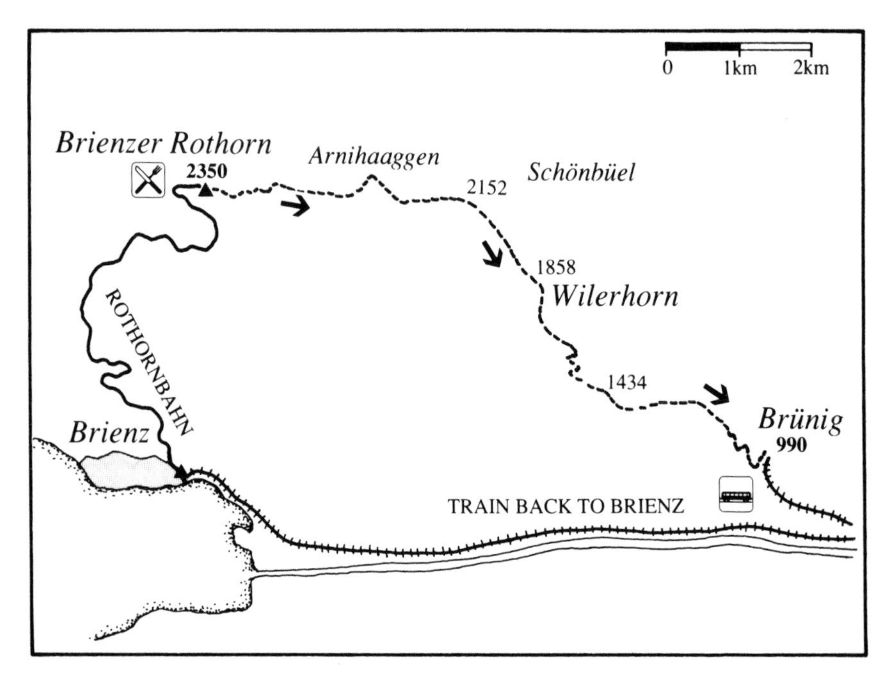

right still the more distant Steghorn, Wildstrubel and Wildhorn are part of the extensive panorama. The entire length of Lake Brienz is visible far below, and so is part of Lake Thun. Pilatus is recognisable to the north-east, while to the east the Titlis and the Sustenhorn are prominent.

Walk down from the summit for a couple of metres then turn left to descend past the Eisee ski lift terminus. Bear right and go down to the Eiseesattel, where there is a four-way junction. Go straight over on a path that you can see ascending the peak ahead. This is a splendid route.

Although there are steep slopes to the left and fixed cables at one point, the situation is not really exposed as the path is comfortably wide. Near the top there is a short stretch of ridge with steep slopes on both sides, but here too the path is fairly wide. You will now be on top of Arnihaaggen (the true summit is a few metres to the right), at 2,207m (7,241ft).

Go on over the peak and descend the zigzags on a path that tends to slope outwards. The mountainside is not so steep on this side. From a col at Zwischenegg (2,086m, 6,842ft) proceed on an almost level path that is first on one side of the ridge then the other. After topping a minor summit the path takes to the south side, and contours exhilaratingly as it faithfully follows each rib and gully.

At a three-way junction on the promontory at Gibel (2,040m, 6,691ft)

A steam train on the Brienzer Rothorn

Arnihaagen from the Rothorn

The Rothorn from the path on Arnihaagen

carry on in the same line. (The left branch goes to a cableway at Schonbuel from where it is possible to descend to Lungern.)Descend a ridge, steep at first, then becoming level and narrowing. There is a short portion where the slopes on each side are steep; you may feel mildly exposed here, but fixed cables have been installed along the crest. Continue down grassy slopes to a col with another junction. Go right and soon you will be on a path that is slanting gently downwards.

At Salewang (1,760m, 5,773ft) a path comes in from the right. Bear left and continue to slant downwards on a narrow *Bergweg*. Where this bears right, down steeper ground, there are many zigzags, but eventually it comes down to a wider track. Turn left along it, still descending but more gradually. Bear right at a junction then right again. After passing a cluster of buildings the track changes character and becomes a narrow, steep, rocky path through woodland. Go through a gate and shortly the path becomes wider and steeper. Go straight over a four-way junction and in a few minutes you will arrive at the main motor road that goes over the Brünig Pass. Turn left and walk up to the top of the pass. The railway station (refreshments available) can be seen ahead on the right of the road.

Footnote It is possible to obtain an all-in ticket that includes the mountain railway and the mainline journey. In 1989 this cost SFr 28.20 (subject to 50 per cent discount to Half Fare Travel Card holders).

Walk 27 Meiringen – Wylerli – Innertkirchen – Aareschlucht – Meiringen

Map nos:	Oberhasli Wanderkarte (1:50,000) Swiss Survey 255 (1:50,000), 1210 (1:25,000)
Walking time:	2 hours 45 minutes
Grading:	Easy walking. No exposure anywhere.
Highest altitude:	Wylerli 829m (2,720ft)
Lowest altitude:	Sand 604m (1,982ft)

The river Aare rises in the vicinity of the Grimsel Pass and flows in a north-westerly direction through the Haslital towards Lake Brienz. On its way it passes through the village of Innertkirchen, and after another 4.8km goes to the south of the town of Meiringen. Between these two places the river runs for almost 1.6km through the Aareschlucht, a fantastic gorge.

The walk starts at Meiringen and climbs up the northern flank of the Haslital to descend through pastureland and forest to Innertkirchen. The return is along the river bank and through the Aareschlucht (admission fee SFr 4).

The Walk

Emerging from Meiringen railway station go right and then left at a T-junction. Go straight across the main street and along to the church with its separate tower. Turn right here and shortly go over a junction and up some steps. You now walk through a small park, crossing a footbridge with an attractive waterfall up to the left. Keep on in the same line as you come to a junction after going up and then down separated flights of steps.

Walk on between residential buildings, and when you are clear of them take the left branch at a fork. This wide path climbs through beech woods then emerges from the trees to pass two barns. It climbs steeply past a chalet then bends right and soon crosses a bridge near the top of a waterfall. Shortly the path passes near the top of a bigger fall then bends sharply left to approach a chalet. The path, now much narrower, arrives at a T-junction. Turn right,

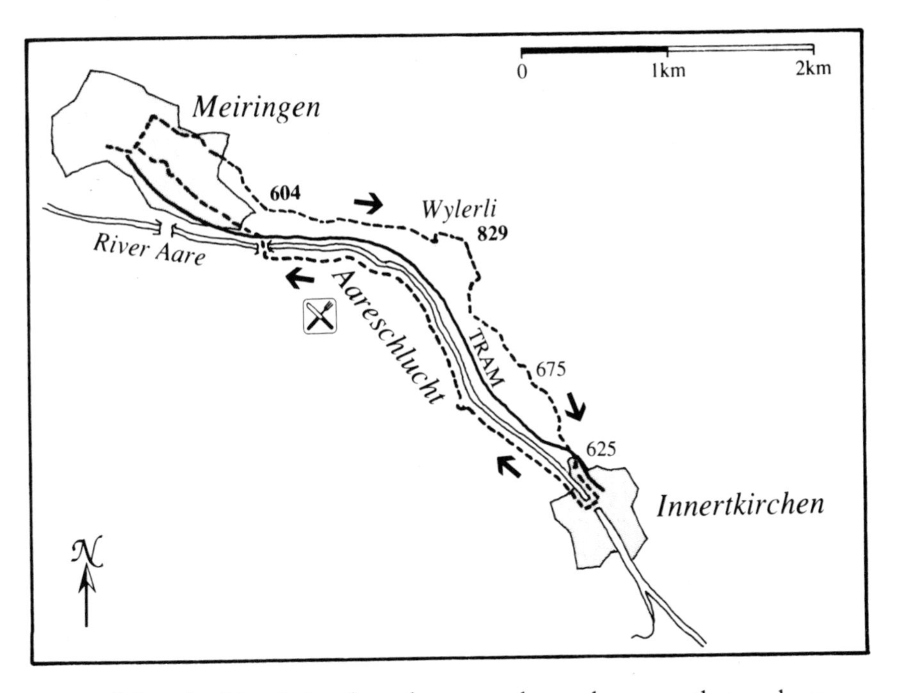

round the side of the chalet, through a gate and cross the stream that produces the waterfall below. Now the path crosses a bank where the bedrock is exposed in places. Soon, bear right, descending slightly to a gate at the edge of a wood. Go down through the trees to emerge on to a forestry road. Turn right and descend, negotiating a number of hairpin bends. At Appigen the road acquires a tarmac surface. Proceed to the bottom right-hand hairpin then bear left to cross the Godmerwasse by means of a covered bridge.

You rejoin the road but leave it again on the right to walk along the side of the river Aare to Innertkirchen. Turn right to cross a road bridge, then right again to walk along the opposite bank of the river. After about quarter of an hour, cross a footbridge over a tributary stream and climb a footpath to the road. The entrance to the Aareschlucht is about 100m up the road to the right.

The admission charge of SFr 4 to walk through the gorge is good value, and the walkways are well protected. However, if there has been recent rain, it is a good idea to have a waterproof with you, as water drips from the overhangs and tunnels. The gorge has been carved by the river through a rocky barrier left here by glacial action countless centuries ago. In places it is of the order of 200m deep.

The walkway begins along the vertical side of a fairly narrow gorge, with

The Aareschlucht

the Aare gushing along at the bottom. It then narrows dramatically, with the river undercutting the rock below. Where it has not been practical to build a walkway, tunnels have been cut through the rock. A point is reached where the gorge widens and a waterfall cascades down from above. Just where you think the best is past, the *Schlucht* becomes even narrower. There is just enough room for a walkway between the rock walls, then tunnels are necessary again. This really is an amazing gorge, and one of the best of its kind.

At the western end, you emerge by a restaurant and walk down the approach road. After 0.5km cross the river by a bridge to the right and immediately turn left. Walk along a straight road to Meiringen, going straight over a junction into the main street. Walk down this and turn left then right to regain the railway station.

If time is short and you wish to cut out the first part of the walk, you can travel to Innertkirchen by means of a tram that operates over an extension to the railway line. From the main railway station go right, then at the T-junction go right again, back to the railway. The tram terminus is along to the left. (Single fare SFr 2.20, subject to 50 per cent discount to holders of the Half Fare Travel Card.)

Walk 28 Engstlenalp – Tannenalp – Erzegg – Balmeregghorn – Planplatten – Reuti

Maps nos:	Oberhasli Wanderkarte (1:50,000) Swiss Survey 255 (1:50,000), 1210 (1:25,000)
Walking time:	5 hours 45 minutes, including visit to Engstlensee
Grading:	Moderate. No significant exposure.
Highest altitude:	Balmeregghorn 2,255m (7,398ft)
Lowest altitude:	Reuti 1,061m (3,481ft)

From Innertkirchen the valley of Gental runs north-east towards the Joch Pass, with the beautiful lake of Engstlensee at its head. In recent years a motor road has been built up the valley, opening up this area to the tourist and walker. Above the north-west side of the Gental is a ridge from Tannensee to Planplatten, above Reuti.

The walk starts from Engstlenalp, visiting the Engstlensee before climbing to Tannen. It then goes up and over Erzegg, along the ridge to the summit of the Balmeregghorn and on to Planplatten. The descent is a circuitous route through pastureland to Reuti.

Engstlenalp can be reached by PTT bus from Meiringen, a pleasant journey that takes 55 minutes.

At the end of the walk you can descend from Reuti to Meiringen in 7 minutes by cable car.

The walk can be shortened by descending from Planplatten to Reuti by a combination of chairlift and gondola cableway. This would reduce the walking time by 2 hours. Correspondingly shorter lengths of time could be saved by descending by gondola from Magisalp or Bidmi.

The Walk

From where the PTT bus stops at Engstlenalp, go out of the end of the car park and walk down to the Engstlensee, a pretty lake cradled in the mountains and reflecting the snowy heights. Go left on a track along the shore and follow it

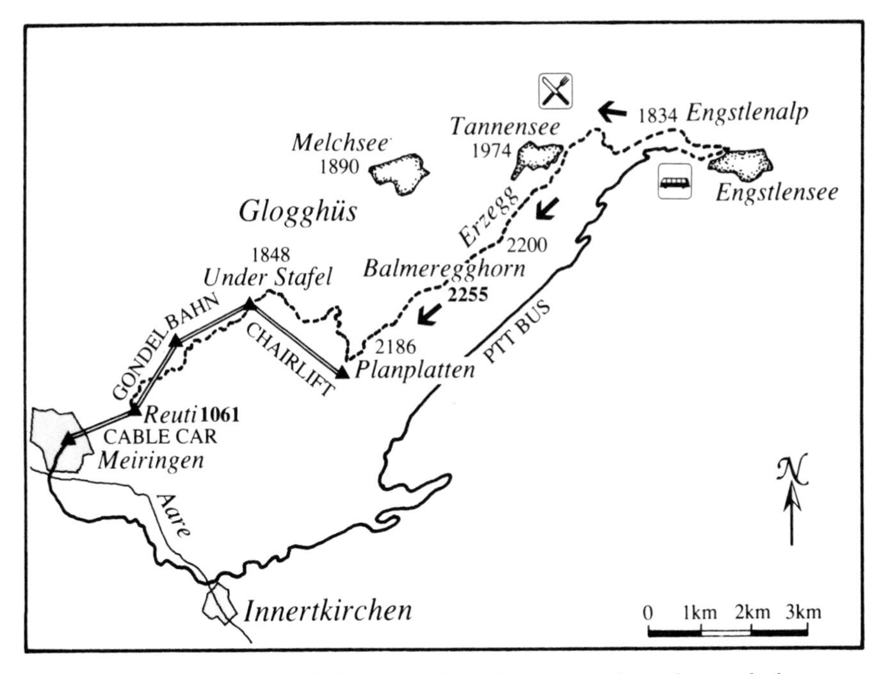

until you come to the path from Joch Pass, that comes along the north shore. Turn left and walk back towards the village of Engstlenalp, turning right by the hotel. This path soon swings left and crosses a stream.

Bear right at a junction then start to climb, steeply at one point. Buildings appear ahead and presently you arrive at Tannenalp. Pass through a rotary stile and walk between the church and the youth hostel, which is also a *Berghaus* (refreshments).

You now find yourself on a macadam road which you follow for a short distance, turning left when you come to a lake, the Tannensee. Walk along the eastern shore on a broad track but on reaching the south-eastern corner of the lake, go left on a *Bergweg*. This now goes directly up the slopes of the Erzegg and is quite steep around the middle of the climb. A large cross with a seat below it marks the top at 2,140m(7,021ft).

Below and to the right, another lake, the Melchsee, has come into view. Looking back, the Engstlensee can be seen in its mountain bowl, with snowy peaks behind, including the Titlis.

Walk on in the same line, on a well-defined path. The ridge becomes more pronounced with the path sometimes on the crest, but generally on the north-west side, just below the edge. In undulates a little but the trend is upward. After one or two false tops, the Balmeregghorn appears ahead with

The Engstlenalpsee from Erzegg

the chairlift from the Melchsee on its right-hand flank. Walk down to a col, go through a rotary stile, then climb the final slopes. The view from the summit is extensive. The Wetterhorn group shows up well to the south-west and to the left of these peaks are the summits of the Schreckhorn and the Finsteraarhorn, although neither shows the sharp profile seen from some other viewpoints. Just north of east, the Titlis can be seen. Nearer at hand, you can look down to Melchsee and its environs.

The descent from the Balmeregghorn to a saddle is quite steep and as you climb the zigzags on the opposite slopes you are no longer on a ridge, but on the side of a mountain called Glockhaus, a rather shapeless mass that seems to be composed of rotten rock. Onward progress is now along a shelf on the mountainside, contouring the steep slopes.

Planplatten and its chairlift appear ahead, but before you come to it you go right through a rotary stile, to descend through pastureland. You may be used to seeing cows grazing high in the Alps during the summer, but here there seems to be more than in most places. There must be hundreds on the slopes through which you now descend. At a junction, bear left and soon you come down to the farm at Hindere Tschuggi. Walk on a road through the buildings, then immediately go right on a path that remains parallel with a stream for a while and then approaches and crosses it. A few metres beyond, you reach a road and bear right down it. At a junction, turn left and walk up towards the Magisalp station of the Reuti cableway.

Almost under the cables bear right, down a road at first then on grass for a considerable distance, gradually drawing away from the cableway. Reaching a road, turn right and walk down it to a T-junction (the Bidmi cableway station is off to the right). Turn left and almost immediately go right, down a path. Go straight over a four-way junction and soon pass under the cableway. Go over another four-way junction and on down to the road at Reuti. Turn left to the cable car station.

Walk 29 Meiringen – Lammi – Geissholz – Reichenbach Falls – Meiringen

Map nos:	Oberhasli Wanderkarte (1:50,000) Swiss Survey 255 (1:50,000), 1210 (1:25,000)
Walking time:	3 hours
Grading:	Moderate. Some of the situations in the vicinity of the falls could be described as exposed.
Highest altitude:	Above Reichenbach Falls approx. 950m (3,117ft)
Lowest altitude:	Meiringen Bridge 602m (1,975ft)

Most people have heard of Sherlock Holmes, and many will be aware that the famous fictional detective and his arch rival Moriarty fell to their supposed deaths from the top of the Reichenbach Falls. There is little doubt that this awe-inspiring waterfall made a great impression on the creator of Holmes, Sir Arthur Conan Doyle, as it has on countless thousands, before and since.

It is located on the southern flank of the Haslital, directly opposite Meiringen and can be included in a pleasant, varied walk that starts and finishes in that town. The route crosses the river Aare at Sand then climbs through wood and meadow to Geissholz. After that it contours the valley flank before descending to the bottom of the falls, then ascends the slopes to the east of the cataract. The walk visits the top of the falls then descends to the valley bottom and back to Meiringen.

The Walk

Walk away from Meiringen railway station to the main street, turn right and walk along to a four-way junction. Go straight over and walk down the straight Sandstrasse to its end where there is a footbridge over the river Aare. Cross the bridge and the road on the other side then go up a path sloping slightly left. There follows a pleasant walk up through woodland. When you reach the top and clear the trees, keep on in the same line and shortly reach

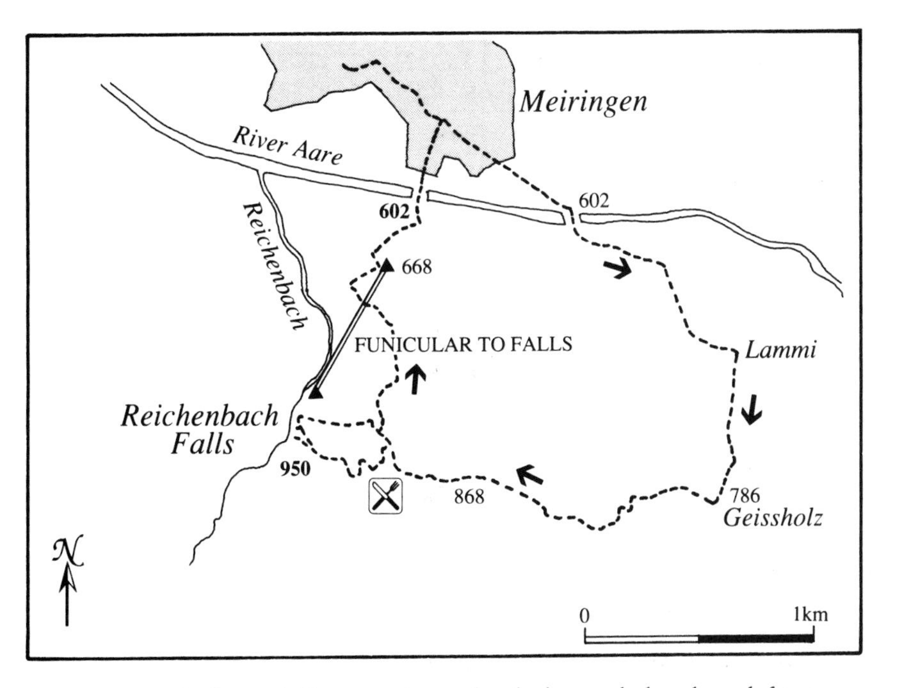

a motor road at Lammi. Go across the road and take a path that slopes left into the trees. When you come to another road go to the right and walk up it for about 150m. Bear left on a path over a field, cross the same road again and walk up the path opposite. When this again meets the road, walk up it into Geissholz. At the end of the village, turn right on a narrow road that becomes a track. When you come to a motor road, go right for a few metres then left on a path. This gives attractive walking through woodland alternating with pastureland, with occasional views of Meiringen in the valley.

Turn right down a narrow lane and soon you come to Hotel Schwendi. Go left on a footpath opposite and climb across a grassy slope towards the Reichenbach Falls. Boards with battens nailed to them are in position to enable you to get close to the bottom of the main fall. The noise of falling water is deafening, the air is filled with a fine spray, when the sun is out a rainbow arcs across the raging stream. You may now go up a steep path, turning aside to the right to view the fall at half height. Return to the path which now veers left through forest and arrives at a T-junction at Tannenhubel (930m, 3,050ft).

Turn right on the wider path still through the forest and walk up until it nears the motor road above. It is now possible to go down a path on the right to a footbridge over the Reichenbach at the top of the fall. The view

The Reichenbach Falls

The Sherlock Holmes Memorial Plaque

downwards is breathtaking and the downdraught of cold air, even on a warm day, is remarkable. A little lower is the platform from which, one imagines, Holmes and Moriarty fell.

From here, if you desire, you can descend further on the west side of the fall and return to the valley bottom by funicular railway.

To complete the walk, retrace your steps up to the road and down to Tannenhubel. Now keep straight on, down the path, which is paved with rather rounded stones and inclined to be steep. Take care if conditions are damp, for these stones can be slippery. Eventually the path comes out into the same lane down which you walked earlier.

Go down it again, but this time bear right just before Hotel Schwendi and walk through an orchard. Follow the path as it descends, passing the road several times as it describes hairpin bends. Finally pass under the funicular railway (opened in 1899) and round to the car park. Make for the exit and turn left to cross the river Aare. Walk on in the same line to the four-way junction that you crossed at the start of the walk. Turn left and retrace your steps to the station.

Walk 30 Reuti – Wasserwendi – Oberegg – Reuti

Map nos:	Oberhasli Wanderkarte (1:50,000) Swiss Survey 255 (1:50,000), 1210 (1:25,000)
Walking time:	2 hours
Grading:	Easy. Only gentle slopes encountered.
Highest altitude:	Approximately 1,360m(4,462ft)
Lowest altitude:	Reuti 1,061m (3,481ft)

The northern flank of the Haslital, in the neighbourhood of Meiringen, rises fairly steeply from the valley bottom then falls back to form a broad terrace which is known as Hasliberg. It is not flat by any means, but the average gradients are more gentle than those below.

This is reasonably easy walking country where the paths wander through woodland, pastureland and the occasional village. This walk is fairly typical of what is available in Hasliberg. It starts and finishes in the developing resort of Reuti which is reached from Meiringen by cable car in 7 minutes. The return fare is SFr 5.20 (subject to 50 per cent discount for Half Fare Travel Card holders).

The Walk

Emerging from Reuti cable car station go right, along the side of a motor road, passing over the Alpbach. A little way beyond this bear right, ascending a wide path over a grassy slope. When it reaches a four-way junction, go straight over, on a path that immediately bends left. An old house here dates from 1591. Pass several other houses and turn right between two of them. This path quickly becomes a grassy track as it ascends a bank, then reverts to a stony path as it enters a wood of mostly broad-leaved trees. Emerging into the open the path levels off with Wasserwendi just ahead at 1,217m (3,993ft). (From the village a cableway rises, in two stages, to the Hochstrass at 2,119m, 6,952ft.)

Go straight over a junction and bear slightly left to 'tee' into a road. Turn right to walk up the road, which at this point is part of the *Panoramaweg.*

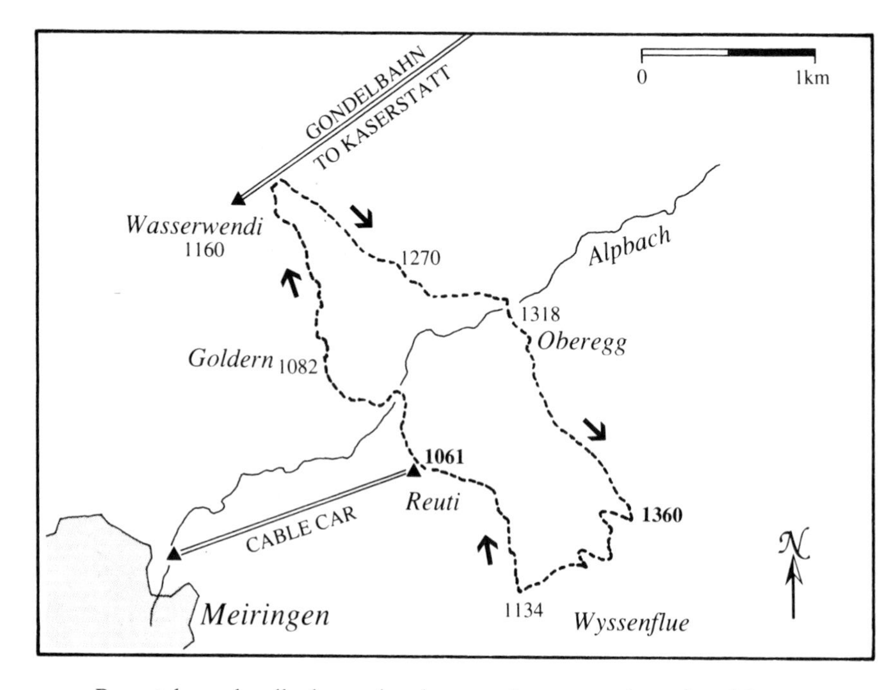

Bear right and walk along a level way with views to the right of the snow-covered Wetterhorn group. The peaks are the Rosenhorn, the Mittelhorn, and the Wetterhorn itself. The lower Wellhorn is in front while the rocky mass to the left is the Engelhorner. To the right of the impressive north face of the Wetterhorn is the gap of Grosse Scheidegg. The mountain mass to the right of that is dominated by the Schwarzhorn.

At the junction of Obersgaden (1,252m, 4,107ft) bear left up a grassy track. Bear right to enter a wood and soon cross a footbridge over the Alpbach. The gondola cableway can be seen ahead. Go under the cables and climb a grassy bank with a wire fence at your right-hand. At the top go over a four-way junction then pass two barns and climb a grassy bank to enter a belt of trees.

After a further open area, a three-bar 'stile' gives access to a wood. Walk through this on a level path which presently descends a little then rises to a junction with a motor road. Turn right and walk down this. You negotiate a number of hairpin bends before turning right on a track, just before the road bridges a stream. The track steepens and acquires a rather loose surface. Finally it 'tees' into a motor road where you turn right and walk along to Reuti.

A chalet at Goldern